A.J. SMITH'S SPORTING CLAYS MASTERCLASS

A.J. SMITH'S SPORTING CLAYS MASTERCLASS

A.J. Smith and Tony Hoare

ARGUS BOOKS

ARGUS BOOKS

Argus House, Boundary Way, Hemel Hempstead,
Hertfordshire HP2 7ST England

First published by Argus Books 1991
© A.J. Smith and Tony Hoare 1991
All photographs by John Best

ISBN 1 85486 049 6

Phototypesetting by Photoprint, Torquay, Devon
Printed and bound in Great Britain by
Clays Ltd, St Ives plc

CONTENTS

FOREWORD

Twice FITASC Sporting Clay World Champion, and winner of numerous other British, US and European Sporting Championships, A.J. 'Smoker' Smith is one of the finest shots in the world today.

During the spring and summer of 1990, I travelled many thousands of miles with A.J. and attended FITASC Sporting competitions in the United Kingdom and Europe with him as we gathered material for this book. When the season started, A.J. was defending his World and European FITASC championship titles. From the outset, he was under intense pressure.

Wherever we went, A.J. was always the centre of attraction. In France, especially, shooters of many different nationalities – French, Italians, Belgians, Germans and many, many Americans – wanted to meet him. He was constantly waylaid and asked his advice – usually by strangers and in broken English – about targets, guns and cartridges.

To his great credit, I never once saw him try to avoid any of these encounters. He remained unfailingly courteous to everyone who approached him and always dispensed advice willingly and with good humour.

One day, when more strangers than usual intercepted him as he walked from one shooting stand to another, I asked him if he ever became irritated by their attention. He was genuinely surprised that I could even consider the question. 'Shooting has given me a wonderful life,' he said. 'I believe I must put as much back into the sport as I possibly can. I *owe* it to these people to stop and speak to them.' It takes a very special personality to tolerate that kind of extraneous pressure when one is about to shoot in defence of a World or European title.

A.J. has long been regarded as a fine ambassador for clay shooting. He certainly confirmed it for me on the shooting grounds of Europe by showing infinite charm and patience to scores of total strangers who wanted just to talk to him and shake his hand.

Tony Hoare

A.J. 'Smoker' Smith.

INTRODUCTION

In my first book, *Sporting Clays*, I set out to provide a comprehensive insight into every facet of English Sporting, which is by far the most popular form of clay pigeon shooting practised in the United Kingdom.

Now, in *Sporting Clays Masterclass*, I am taking that instruction further. In this book I describe in detail the types of target encountered in the more advanced and complex discipline of FITASC – or International – Sporting. I also give full explanations of the different formats for FITASC Sporting shooting and discuss fully the pros and cons of what are now universally known as the 'new' and 'old' systems.

FITASC is undoubtedly my favourite shooting discipline. I sincerely hope that by giving you an insight into its enduring excitement and never-ending challenge, you too will come to appreciate and enjoy it as much as I do. The essential difference between FITASC and English Sporting lies in the way certain combinations of targets are presented as 'doubles' but, in many ways, the basic approach to single targets is just the same as in English Sporting. For this reason, I recommend that the *Masterclass* is read in conjunction with *Sporting Clays*.

Finally I would like to thank Tony Hoare for his invaluable assistance in the preparation of this book. Tony, who is a keen clay shot, was a senior editorial executive in national newspapers for many years before launching his own public relations and media consultancy.

I hope you have as much enjoyment reading *Masterclass* as we had preparing it.

A.J. Smith

CHAPTER ONE

THE BEGINNING

I can recall as though it was yesterday the very first time I shot FITASC Sporting. In fact it was many years ago, on a warm spring day in 1980 at Alec Bonnett's lovely ground at Ware in Hertfordshire, England.

Since then I must have shot more than 50,000 targets in FITASC competitions all over the world, but to this day that initial 100-bird competition is etched indelibly in my memory. I can remember being absolutely enthralled and excited by the quality and variety of the targets on each of the four layouts.

As a trap and sporting shooter who had been in World championship and British Commonwealth Games teams, I had heard a lot about the unique characteristics of FITASC Sporting. However, I had dismissed the French enthusiasm for it as Gallic exaggeration – after all, how *could* any sporting discipline better the home-grown English variety?

The answer was emphatic and lay in the targets I shot that late March day at Ware. They were a revelation, like no others I had ever encountered – an electrifying variety of singles and doubles which offered the ultimate test of shooting ability. After one 25-bird layout I was converted, and my respect and passion for FITASC remains undiminished, a decade and many thousands of targets later. It is, in my opinion, the most complete and unforgiving form of clay competition, the ultimate test of the pure *art* of shooting.

Although I would never have dreamt it then, that shoot in Hertfordshire was to change the course of my life. It was the starting point for an exciting and often gruelling route to the Great Britain team, to two World and three European championship titles and countless other victories in international competition throughout Europe and the United States. I am proud to say that on the way to those World and European successes I have competed against and beaten the very best at FITASC from every shooting nation.

(*Above*) Great Britain squad and (*below*) US Sporting Clays
Association's international team at the 1990 World FITASC
championships in France, 1990.

I am joint holder, with that great Belgian shooter and former World champion Marc Polet, of the world record score for FITASC, a feat accomplished when I won the European championship for the first time at Vilamoura in Portugal in 1984. My score for that formidable 200-bird competition was 190 – five targets ahead of second-placed French FITASC ace Michel Riboulet.

Every year I travel over 80,000 miles by road and air throughout the UK and to Austria, France, Germany, Belgium, Switzerland, Portugal and the USA, either to compete or to coach. In each country I visit I see evidence of the enormous growth in the popularity of FITASC. More and more people are shooting it in every country, every year.

It has been especially heartening in the last couple of years to witness the tremendous interest in clay shooting which is being generated in the United States. English Sporting is sweeping the entire country, from New York to California, and from Chicago to Florida. The ever-ambitious Americans are already organising FITASC competitions and the country's top shooters are visiting Europe to gain experience of the discipline by participating in major shoots.

America has been fiercely competitive at skeet and trap on the world stage for many years, and two teams of their first-rate sporting shooters attended the 1990 FITASC World championships at Le Rabot in France, one from the US Sporting Clays Association and the other representing the breakaway National Sporting Clays Association. World-class competitors, like Dan Carlisle and Jon Kruger, made the trans-atlantic crossing to sample the outstanding French targets at Le Rabot, where the record entry of 720 shooters from a dozen nations was further evidence of FITASC's astonishing growth.

As shooters of the calibre of Carlisle and Kruger experience FITASC on its 'home' grounds and take their experience back to America, it surely won't be long before the Americans themselves are staging inter-national FITASC competitions of the highest quality. When you consider that twenty million Americans have firearms licences, it doesn't take much imagination to realise the enormous potential for the sport's growth and development. Already, shooting grounds in Florida, New York and Colorado Springs have staged excellent competitions. I won the first of them in Florida, and the second at New York's Pawling Mountain Gun Club. The targets at Pawling Mountain were as challenging as anything I have experienced in Europe, and that has to be very encouraging for the future of FITASC in the United States.

Bear in mind, too, that the Americans are prepared to inject large sums of money into the sport and also have the space to stage satisfactory events under the 'new' FITASC system. I am sure it will only be a few years before we witness the emergence of a whole new crop of resolute world-class performers – wearing the Stars and Stripes on their skeet vests!

The Japanese and Brazilians are two more nations who have recently discovered the delights, frustrations and great spirit of international competition in FITASC. I am sure that, as its reputation and popularity gathers pace, all the world's shooting nations will adopt the discipline. When they do, they will pose a very real threat to the British and French stranglehold on the World and European titles. FITASC is at last becoming a truly international discipline, rather than just a European one.

What is FITASC?

So what is FITASC, the organisation which has given its name to this most exciting form of clay pigeon shooting?

The Fédération Internationale de Tir Aux Armes Sportives de Chasse, to give it its full title, has headquarters in Paris and is one of two organisations responsible for international shooting disciplines. The other is the International Shooting Union (ISU), which governs the Olympic shooting disciplines of trench and skeet, as well as competitive pistol and rifle shooting.

FITASC, which has 51 member federations from 47 countries, was created in 1921 as the International Union of Shooting. Its aim was to unite the world's clay shooting organisations. It changed its name to FITASC in 1936 and by 1940 was regularly organising international skeet and trench events and World championships. In 1947, it conceded the skeet and trench (fifteen trap) disciplines to the ISU – at that time already a member of the Olympic Committee – so that they could be included in the Olympic Games. Today FITASC is responsible for developing all the other international disciplines, such as Sporting, Universal Trench (five trap) and Automatic Ball Trap.

In 1953, the ISU and FITASC signed an agreement which enabled FITASC to organise annual international competitions and a European championship open to all shooters, while the ISU retained the Olympic Games and World championships. This move gave international clay shooting a tremendous boost as FITASC pursued a policy of staging open international competitions, unlike the ISU's 'closed' World championships and Olympic events which are controlled by strict selection procedures.

FITASC has staged its own open World championships for sporting since 1979, and their competitions have given all clay shooters the opportunity to compete at the highest level. It was in the late 1960s that

Mickey Rouse won everything in sight at FITASC in 1990 –
the European and World championships and the World
Cup. It was an incredible season for one of the nicest
people in shooting.

the first FITASC sporting shoots were staged in the United Kingdom when the discipline was pioneered here by two legendary shooters, Bob Armistead and Stan 'Tiny' Barlow, both of whom are sadly now dead.

Bob, from North Yorkshire, and Tiny, who came from Essex, were trap shooting in France when they first witnessed FITASC Sporting. To their eternal credit, both men immediately recognised its rich potential, and they returned to Great Britain full of enthusiasm for what they had seen.

Bob travelled to France several times to learn more about how to shoot and to stage the discipline. When he and Tiny started to put on their own FITASC competitions on the land Bob farmed in North Yorkshire, entries in those early days rarely exceeded 40 guns. But Bob and Tiny's extraordinary foresight was laying the surest foundations for the success that continues to this day for Great Britain's FITASC shooters.

Once I had experienced the excitement and challenge of FITASC at Alec Bonnett's ground, I dedicated myself wholeheartedly to the discipline. There wasn't a single weekend when I did not participate in a FITASC competition somewhere in the UK, and I ended that exhilarating first year of competitive FITASC by winning the English FITASC Sporting Grand Prix. During the following season I travelled as often as I could to venues throughout France and Belgium, seeking experience of the harder targets encountered at that time on the excellent European layouts.

The sport was dominated then by legendary European FITASC shooters like Belgium's Marc Polet and the French star Michel Riboulet. It wasn't long, however, before the British stamped their authority on the discipline at the highest level and in the most decisive and compelling way. That fine English Sporting shot, Duncan Lawton, from Staffordshire, won the World championship in Madrid in 1981 – and his victory was a categoric declaration to the French and Belgians that their supremacy was at an end.

Duncan's triumph was the forerunner of numerous British victories on the world stage. He had already won the European championship, along with people like Wally Sykes, Brian Hebditch, Brian Wells and Paddy Howe. It wasn't long before Britain had another World champion – Gerry Cowler won it in 1984 in South Africa – and a year later the outstanding Barry Simpson triumphed when the competition was staged at Wynyard Park in County Durham. Since then, British shooters have had an almost unassailable grip on the major international trophies. I have won the World championship twice – the only British shooter to have done so – while Suffolk's John Bidwell and Mickey Rouse, from Oxford, have also won it.

If anything, British ladies have been even more successful, the remarkable Anthea Hillyer and Denise Eyre winning the World title an

The European championship has so far eluded John
Bidwell, although he won the World title in Australia in 1988.

Here I am with George Digweed. George has been a very successful English Sporting shot and I fully expect him to make his presence felt in FITASC in the next couple of seasons.

astonishing nine times between them! Anthea, from Somerset, first won the World championship in 1980 in France and exactly ten years later she won it in France again – having been World champion an unbelievable four times in between! Hers is a truly inspiring record.

Recently, British successes have been equally impressive in European championships, where I have taken the title three times, and Barry Simpson and Duane Morley have also been victorious. Anthea and Denise have also won the European ladies title, and so has Scotland's Ruth Leah. In 1990, the phenomenal, fast-shooting Mickey Rouse won both the World and European championships as well as the FITASC World Cup in a single season of truly amazing and consistent shooting. Britain is also fortunate in having a handful of juniors who are now beginning to win World and European championships. Some are already turning in scores that many seniors would envy and, if their early potential is realised, a whole new crop of world-class competitors will emerge and flourish in the not too distant future.

Britain's international success in recent years has been prodigious, and it is interesting to consider that all the successful FITASC shooters share a single common denominator: all have previously excelled at English Sporting. I have not the slightest doubt that this formidable success in FITASC is a direct consequence of the thorough grounding of British shooters in domestic sporting.

The key to successful FITASC shooting is mastery of the doubles on each shooting stand. It is the combination of two individual targets, either simultaneously, as a following pair or on report, which can test a competitor's overall shooting ability to the absolute limit. Take my word for it, there is certainly no other form of shooting which prepares a shooter for FITASC doubles as comprehensively as English Sporting does.

In a 100-bird English Sporting shoot there will probably be ten stands of ten targets each and, more often than not, each combination of ten targets will be thrown as five doubles of one type or another. Consequently, British Sporting shooters are so familiar with doubles that

Barry Simpson was the World FITASC champion in 1985 and European champion a year later. He is always a particularly resolute opponent.

they remain unperturbed when they encounter them. The French, Belgians and Swiss, however, do not have an equivalent of English Sporting so, when they are confronted by doubles on a FITASC layout, they find them much harder to cope with than do the British.

However, I believe the Americans will find it easier to adapt to FITASC. As I said earlier, English Sporting is popular throughout the United States and most American shooters are cutting their clay teeth on English Sporting targets before moving on to FITASC. They will have learned, just as we did, how to tackle doubles before they ever encounter them on FITASC layouts. I am certain the experience will be of great benefit to them.

Because I have been so successful at the highest level in trap and sporting shooting, I am often asked which discipline I believe is the hardest to shoot.

I was a member of the 1978 Commonwealth Games Olympic trap squad, and also shot in the Great Britain trench team in the World championship at Seoul in South Korea. I know that many people believe that Olympic trench, with its acoustically-released 90 mile-an-hour targets and fifteen traps – three for each shooting peg – is the most difficult discipline of all.

There is certainly a feeling among many top trench shooters that theirs is the cream of all the disciplines, and the most demanding because of its sheer intensity and the breathtaking speed and acute angles of the targets. I would agree that trench shooting requires the most extraordinary concentration – the ability to kill similar targets repeatedly calls for acute mental preparation. But, as a test of pure shooting ability, trench can never compare with FITASC.

Although the trajectory of every trench bird varies according to the way it leaves the trap, all the targets basically go away from the shooter, so the type of bird presented is inevitably limited. It is because of FITASC's abundant variety of targets that it reigns supreme over every other discipline. For instance, in one 200-bird competition a shooter can be faced with 150 completely different targets as singles or doubles, any one of which will punish even the slightest shooting error.

Where trench is a discipline which can be taught, FITASC favours the natural shot: the shooter who does everything correctly and instinctively for each and every target, irrespective of its speed or angle. Having said that, I am convinced that trench has benefited my sporting shooting by teaching me how to concentrate at will, an attribute which has certainly gained me many targets in competition.

When you consider that a margin as narrow as five targets can separate the top twenty shooters in international sporting competitions, you will realise how vital it is to be able to concentrate on each and

This is an example of the superb technique which has made Anthea Hillyer the most successful woman FITASC shot ever. She has been World champion an incredible six times and is shooting better than ever.

Alistair Evans shot some outstanding scores as a junior and it will be interesting to watch his progress now that he has moved up to the seniors.

every bird. One momentary lapse can mean a lost target – and the difference between being a World champion and an also-ran!

Although I was an AA class shooter at English Sporting and qualified for the England team in my first season of competitive clay shooting, I often had trouble maintaining my concentration. I had a tendency to allow my application to waver between shooting stands when I was chatting and joking with friends. As a result, I was not always prepared mentally for the targets which followed, and it certainly cost me birds. When I switched from sporting to trench in 1976, I very quickly realised the supreme importance of self-discipline, of the need for absolute concentration on every single bird in a round of 25 targets.

Lack of concentration is a vicious circle. I would stand on a shooting peg on a trench layout waiting to shoot and my mind would wander. Then, suddenly, it was my turn – and I wasn't prepared. I would mount my gun, call for the bird – and miss! When I moved to the next peg I was still wondering how I had missed and, before I had cleared my mind, it was my turn to shoot again. Because I had been fretting over the bird I had missed, I was still not concentrating – and the chances were that I would miss the next bird too!

Those costly lessons at trench taught me to close my mind to everything but the targets. They instilled in me how important it is never to hark back to a lost bird, but rather to concentrate exclusively on the one you are about to shoot. Worrying about a lost target is a sure-fire recipe for missing the next one. People miss targets for a variety of reasons, and no-one will ever shoot the perfect score at FITASC.

I know that I can kill any bird, and that there isn't a target I can't hit or haven't shot at before, so I never ever hark back to one I have missed. If I miss, it is because I did something wrong, and to let it play on my mind would guarantee even more misses.

Today, I am still very relaxed between shooting stands but, once I am in position and preparing to shoot, experience has taught me to banish everything from my mind but the bird I am about to call for. Concentration comes with experience and confidence in your shooting ability, and no matter how experienced you are it is absolutely vital. Never forget that at FITASC the targets are so varied in terms of speed and angle that they will find any chink in your shooting armour.

I have shot for so long now that I know immediately the birds I will find easy and those which will be more difficult, and I instinctively concentrate more intently on the harder ones. When I am shooting a target that I consider will be difficult for me, I will shut my gun, point it in the particular place I have selected to pick up the bird and then really think about the target before calling for it. On the easier ones,

The referee shows the targets to the first shooter on a FITASC squad. The shooter in question is Brian Hebditch, a very well known sporting FITASC performer.

everything happens a little more quickly although I am still concentrating and bringing years of experience to bear on the bird in question.

As you gain experience, you learn to concentrate at a different level on the birds you believe will be difficult, and less intently on the bread-and-butter targets you know you will kill. I must stress that the ability to vary the intensity of concentration only comes with experience and shooters who are still developing their knowledge and technique should concentrate as hard as they can on *every* target.

It is surely a real indication of the severity and challenge of FITASC targets that, almost 20 years after I first started shooting English Sporting, and a decade on from my first FITASC event, the sport is still dominated by the same shooters. The competitors who were always in contention when I entered sporting are still there today – Barry Simpson, John Bidwell and, perhaps to a lesser extent recently, Paddy Howe.

Because it is a discipline which favours the natural shot, it is very rare for anyone to develop through the ranks at FITASC. Occasionally, a youngster enters the sport and presents a real challenge to the established names immediately, but those who do – like the prodigiously talented Stevie Whitelock – are shooters with inherent natural talent. They shoot senior scores while they are still performing as juniors and there is no protracted learning curve.

In FITASC, you either have the natural shooting talent to succeed at the top or you haven't. Because you are reasonably proficient at English Sporting, it doesn't mean that you can walk on to a FITASC layout and start recording comparable scores. The variety of singles and doubles, the diverse combinations of speed and angle and the taxing mixture of midis, minis, battues and rockets will provide targets you have never experienced before.

If you genuinely love shooting, there is no finer discipline, and FITASC can become a consuming and absolute passion. It certainly captivated me for life on that spring day all those years ago at Alec Bonnett's shooting ground.

CHAPTER TWO

FITASC OLD AND NEW

Paradoxically, the exceptional growth in the popularity of FITASC Sporting throughout Europe and in other parts of the world, has presented the sport's administrators with very real problems.

If it is shot as it was originally devised, under what is now known as the 'old' system, FITASC competition must be restricted to 144 shooters, the maximum number of guns which can be catered for in a single day. Faced with the increasing number of people wishing to shoot the discipline, FITASC officials were forced to go back to the drawing board in 1987 to devise a system which would enable more shooters to participate in less time. As a result, the 'new' straight-through system was introduced, and with it there were considerable changes to the actual shooting format.

It was greeted with widespread disapproval and there has been harsh criticism by some international performers who feel that the changes have robbed FITASC shooting of the very qualities which made it so special to them. Nevertheless, all major competitions are now organised under the straight-through system, and grounds are successfully coping with much larger entries as a result.

There would have been no-one happier than I if FITASC could have continued under the old system. But as it was quite clear that it couldn't, I supported the change to allow more people to shoot it. I believe it would have been very selfish for people like me, who know and have shot both systems, to have insisted on it staying as it was, and thereby effectively prevent a lot of other people from taking part.

The outcome would have been that international FITASC competitions

I always position my feet facing the spot where I have
chosen to shoot the target, and then swing my body back
to pick up the bird visually as early as possible.

This a similar stance from another angle. Again, I have placed my feet towards the area where I will shoot the target and have swung back with my body to pick up the bird as soon as I possibly can. This also ensures that I have a fluent swing.

would have gone the way of trap and skeet, and countries would have had to qualify to send a number of shooters to competitions like the World or European championships. They would no longer have been open competitions.

That is not what FITASC is all about. It has been supported for many years by a large and faithful contingent of shooters, particularly the British, who have travelled all over Europe participating at their own expense, purely for the pleasure of shooting such superb targets.

Many of the most ardent supporters of FITASC have never had any hope of winning at all, but they have still continued to travel thousands of miles every year shooting it. If we had stayed on the old system, many of those shooters who have supported FITASC right from the beginning would have been victimised and unable to shoot it in the future.

As the numbers for FITASC keep on growing, I do believe it is imperative that all the people who wish to shoot it are accommodated and given the opportunity to do so. If that means that things have to change for those of us who have been fortunate enough to shoot it for years, then so be it.

It is a fact, however, that most people who have shot the two systems do prefer the original, and many smaller events are still run under it.

The Old System

This is organised around a 25-bird layout consisting of three shooting stands and four or five hidden traps. On a good layout, the angle and direction of the targets alter considerably as the shooters move from one stand to another.

For instance, a high going-away bird on stand one may be a driven on stand three. A left to right crosser on stand two could be a right to left on stand three – the permutations are numerous and lie at the very heart of a good FITASC event.

Shooters are grouped into numbered squads of six, either by draw or computer, before the event begins and shoot each layout at a pre-determined time. There will be a notice in the club-house telling you what time your squad is to shoot a particular layout. When the shooters arrive at the first shooting stand on a layout, the referee will show the squad the targets before shooting begins. Shooting is in strict rotation, starting with the single targets on stand one.

These are shot in the order the shooters are listed on the scorecard: 1 2 3 4 5 6. The stand one doubles follow, shot first by shooter No 2 and then by 3 4 5 6 1. The squad then moves on to stand two, and the singles there are shot first by shooter No 3 followed by 4 5 6 1 2.

Doubles start with shooter No 4, and so on. It is usual to shoot four singles and two doubles on each stand, with an extra single on one of them, so the total for the layout is 25 targets.

Under the old system, only one squad is allowed on a layout at any one time, so two shooting stands remain vacant while a squad is shooting the third.

The New System

The new system has been described by its critics as nothing more than 'squadded' English Sporting. True, there were some serious difficulties when it was first introduced, mainly because the targets were not as varied and exciting as previously. Since then, however, the French and Cypriots have demonstrated, in World and European championships, that with enough space the new system can be just as challenging and enjoyable as the old.

Under the new system, each stand on a particular layout is completely separate, very similar at first sight to those encountered on an English Sporting layout. Unlike English Sporting, however, it will have up to seven traps to produce the target variation required for FITASC.

It will also have its own referee and scorer and, as soon as one squad has shot and moved on to another self-contained stand, another six shooters immediately take their place. There are usually four stands to a layout and every one is constantly occupied – unlike the old system where two stands were always vacant as the third was being shot. This method of shooting FITASC requires a lot of space, so that targets can be thrown safely in every direction while shooting is proceeding simultaneously on other stands on the layout.

At the World championships at Le Rabot in 1990, the French demonstrated how successfully the new system can handle large numbers of shooters by putting 120 squads through eight layouts in less than three days. It was a remarkable organisational feat and, because the shooting ground at Le Rabot covers such a vast area, it was achieved without resorting to inferior targets. The birds were certainly up to the high standard we have come to expect from the French in major competitions.

It was a similar story at the European championships in Cyprus where the targets were also outstanding. The Cypriots, too, demonstrated how enjoyable the new system can be when space is not a restricting factor.

Criticisms of the initial shoots under the new system were mainly about target variety – most of the birds tended to be going-away or quartering, and I think that this was the result of inexperience or lack of

Here I am preparing to shoot a high, crossing bird straight out in front. I have turned to follow the line of the bird from the moment it appears.

Now the bird is in a position to shoot. I have swung on to
it and mounted and am about to fire.

space. If the quality and variety of targets is maintained, I cannot see any disadvantages at all with the new system, although there are obviously some facets of the old that I miss.

One advantage of the old system is that you are able to read the birds on the different stands on a layout and you can decide where they might be shot subsequently.

After I had shot the targets on stand one under the old system, I always worked out where I was going kill them on stands two and three. It was possible to develop a rare insight into the birds as you moved around the stands shooting the same targets from different positions. To me, that was one of the outstanding qualities of FITASC – reading every single target from the position you were shooting it and then trying to interpret the variation in its flight accurately from stand to stand. Because each stand is quite separate under the new system, you don't have the same opportunity to analyse the targets.

The Basics

Whether it's under the new system or the old, however, a shooter's first experience of FITASC can be quite nerve-racking and some highly proficient sporting shots take many months to perform confidently at FITASC.

Although your scores will probably drop when you first start shooting it, it is important not to be intimidated by the aura which has grown up around FITASC. Indeed, some shooters are literally frightened off by its mystique. Rest assured: if you are a reasonably experienced and competent English Sporting shot, there is no reason why you should not *eventually* record respectable scores at FITASC.

At the beginning, try to relax and savour the enjoyment of shooting the greater variety of targets. Instead of shooting five pairs of one particular target, as you do in English Sporting, you will shoot ten different birds. In English Sporting, FITASC targets must only account for 30 per cent of the birds, and I am certain you will appreciate the preponderance of minis, midis, battues, rockets and rabbits you will shoot at in FITASC.

If you appreciate shooting as an art in its own right, you will certainly grow to appreciate FITASC and, as you do, you will gain confidence and your scores will begin to improve. But don't expect it to happen instantly, and do be prepared to persevere if you find it hard going at the beginning. You won't be the first shooter to consider taking up golf after your first few outings at FITASC!

The most tangible difference in FITASC is that targets must be called

The gun is still out of my shoulder as I watch for the appearance of the target, coming high from my right.

for gun down. A rule introduced in 1991 stipulates that to ensure consistency, shooters must wear a distinctive tape on their jackets and the gun stock must be below it in the 'ready' position.

When I first started clay shooting at the beginning of the 1970s, the rule was that English Sporting had to be shot gun down and I have never shot any other way. Nor do I feel that shooting gun up offers the slightest advantage. To shoot with your gun down is far more natural. It affords full vision over your gun, and that enables you to pick up the target, get your gun moving as you mount, swing through and fire. The hardest thing to do is to swing on to a target with the gun in your shoulder – it is unnatural and lacks the fluency necessary to kill targets consistently. And don't try to tell me that having the gun up gives you more time to get on to the bird – it is amazing how quickly you can mount if you are prepared to work at it.

I used to practise consistent mounting at home by picking a spot on the wall, closing my eyes, and then bringing the gun into my shoulder. By doing this frequently, I used to find when I opened my eyes that I was pointing directly at the spot I had chosen. That is perfect gun mounting and, once you have mastered that, all you have to do is concentrate totally on the target. If your eyes are in the right place, your gun will be too.

If further confirmation is required that mounting can be both fast and accurate, consider the fact that I have shot 25 straight at Olympic trench with the gun down – and those trap targets were certainly moving!

Not only must the targets in FITASC be called for gun down, it is also against the rules to move *before* you have *seen* the target. It is essential, therefore, that you never make the mistake of mounting in anticipation, or when you have heard the trap but are unable to see the bird. You must always keep the gun down until the target is in sight.

There will probably be a lot on your mind when you first start shooting FITASC, so it will be tremendously helpful if you study the people in front of you and watch where they kill particular birds. As I explained earlier, FITASC is shot in strict rotation so if you do have to shoot the singles first it can be a disadvantage – the only opportunity you will get to see the birds will be when they are shown to you by the referee. However, because you shot the singles first, you will be last on the doubles. Make sure that you take full advantage and watch the five other members of your squad shoot the doubles before you. It should give you a clear indication of the best way to string the birds together to kill them both.

Find out if there are any very experienced shooters in your squad, see where they are looking for the birds, where they are pointing their gun and picking up the targets and exactly where they shoot them.

I always try to stay as relaxed as I possibly can when I am calling for a bird. Once you tense your body, it seriously inhibits your swing. Although I am relaxed, you can see I am concentrating hard.

Totally relaxed again as I wait for a target, but don't be fooled! I am giving the emerging bird 100 per cent concentration.

Remember, too, that you do have full use of the gun on the singles, so always be prepared to second barrel a target which you miss with your first shot.

Never forget that the singles on a FITASC layout are your bread and butter, the doubles being the cream. To start to record a good score, you must kill all the singles, but in doing so you must kill them in such a way that you are already preparing to tackle them as doubles. In other words, you will decide to kill one bird in a particular spot because to kill it there later, when it is the first target of a pair on the doubles, will put you in the best possible position for killing the second bird.

There are tricks which can make an easy bird a little more difficult but leave you in a better position to make the hard bird which follows just a little easier!

This is where we come back to reading the birds. I cannot stress enough how important this is in FITASC. Where you may have three or four pairs of the same birds on one stand in English Sporting, in FITASC you never have the chance to repeat a target. You shoot it in the singles and in the doubles and, if you read it incorrectly, you're in trouble. There are no second chances.

To set about building up a competitive score you must systematically prepare for all the targets, and constantly think ahead from the singles to the doubles. By doing this religiously, you can gain an extra bird on a layout. Competition is fierce, and FITASC is all about shooting 190 when the previous person has shot 189. The way to gain that all-important extra bird is to prepare in advance so that you are shooting the single targets in a way that will be of benefit when you shoot them as doubles.

It is crucial to start building up a score right from the beginning and the way to do it is by attention to detail, by thorough preparation on every stand and, of course, by utter concentration.

If you take the trouble to inspect the scores in major FITASC champion-ships, you will see just how tight competition really is. The 1990 World championship, for instance, was won by Mickey Rouse with a score of 187. Three former World champions — John Bidwell, Marc Polet and I – finished joint sixth and we were only *seven* birds behind Mickey!

Even the fifteenth-placed shooter was only ten birds behind, and the winning *junior* scored a splendid 174. That gives you an idea of the intense competition at the top. To be only seven targets behind the winner in a 200-bird competition seems very close, but the stark truth is that I might as well have been 70 birds behind!

Starting out at FITASC can be quite difficult because there are not so many competitions staged as there are in English Sporting, and it may be that you will have to travel quite a distance to find a shoot. However, there is evidence that more FITASC shoots are being organised up and

These three pictures (*see also pages 40 and 41*) are a
perfect illustration of watching for the bird and then
mounting smoothly to kill it.

I am in the 'ready' position as I call for the bird, carefully
watching the area it will come from.

The bird has entered my vision so I start to bring the gun
into my shoulder as I follow its flight path.

The gun is settled into my shoulder as I prepare to fire.

down the UK as it becomes more popular. Although it is not easy to set up, FITASC does have certain advantages for shoot organisers. It is squadded, and therefore always has to be pre-booked, and most grounds insist on the entry fee with the booking – a move which usually guarantees a full turn-out.

It is, however, considerably more expensive to enter competitions – in the UK, where it may cost £20 for a round of 100 English Sporting, you will probably pay at least twice that for the same number of FITASC targets. The additional expense comes as a surprise to many FITASC first-timers, but considering that there are qualified referees on each layout, more trappers and far more organisation involved, I think the cost in most cases is more than justified.

If you are a member of the Clay Pigeon Shooting Association and want to enter registered FITASC shoots, it is worth noting that the classification percentages for FITASC are slightly different to those for English Sporting. Nor is there an AA class. The classification is as follows: Class A 75 per cent and over. Class B 66 per cent and under 75 per cent. Class C under 66 per cent.

So long as the people who are setting up FITASC shoots are experienced in the discipline themselves and have the facilities to present suitable targets, I think the growth in the number of events is to be applauded. After all, who knows how many future champions are out there waiting to be discovered?

CHAPTER THREE

TANTALISING TARGETS

Before I examine specific layouts under each system, and consider in detail how to shoot the particular targets, I'd like to answer a question I am often asked – what type of gun and cartridge should you use when you start shooting FITASC?

The answer is quite simple. The gun you are happiest with, the one that suits you and with which you shoot well, will be perfectly adequate and is the one you should use. There is no magic gun specifically designed for FITASC targets. If you shoot English Sporting successfully with 28-inch barrels and chokes of a quarter and a half, stick to that combination.

It has become apparent over the years that longer barrels do afford more pointability and, as a result, there has been a tendency for some of the top international sporting shooters to use 32-inch barrels.

I have used them for a few years now and personally I feel that by doing so I am able to achieve a better swing on the more distant targets one tends to encounter at FITASC. I also find that I can point out distant birds with the longer barrels on my Classic Doubles sporter far more easily than with shorter ones, and that they also help me to keep my swing moving more smoothly. The longer barrels appear to give a lot more contact with the target, and I definitely have more control over the relationship between the gun and the bird. Pointability does not apply when you are swinging on to quick, close targets and there are times when the extra barrel length is a slight disadvantage.

Very occasionally, there may be a fast driven partridge which the extra couple of inches make more difficult to tackle, but it is quite possible to swing a long gun just as quickly as a shorter one, although you do have to put a little more effort into it. Although there can be a slight disadvantage on low, fast targets, I do believe the advantages outweigh the drawbacks.

In FITASC, generally, you tend to get targets which are farther away than in English Sporting, and a lot of the more difficult birds in the doubles are on report. This gives you the time to get on to the second bird – in other words, there should be no need to race after them as is so often the case with all the simultaneous doubles encountered in English Sporting. That is where pointability comes into its own. When you are shooting two separate, comparatively long birds, you are not rushed into doing anything silly because you know that you have the time to pick out the target with a longer gun.

As for cartridges, I always use Winchester Winner No 8s and have never felt at the slightest disadvantage by having only one size of cartridge with me in a competition. When one considers the amount of money that is spent by cartridge companies on research, I accept that there must be an advantage somewhere along the line in having a skeet cartridge for, say, a close in target, and a trap cartridge for another bird which is farther away. I am sure there must have been times when I have shot at a target so far out that a No 8 was incapable of breaking it, but I have also killed birds at exceptional distances with 8s.

I am a great believer in keeping shooting as simple as possible. It is a mistake to get too wrapped up in all the technical details surrounding the sport. It follows, therefore, that if I am on a stand with a fixed choke gun and only one size of cartridge, my only concern is hitting the bird, and that is exactly what I am concentrating on. I believe that you are far better off watching the target and deciding where you are going to kill it than worrying if your chokes are correct – or which cartridge you should be selecting.

Some people get far too bogged down with extraneous detail. First they worry about their chokes. Then they wonder if they have the right cartridges – some of them even add another dimension. They start worrying about what colour lenses they should be using in their shooting glasses! By the time they have wrestled with that one, it's time to shoot.

When they address the target they still have so much on their mind – have I got the combination of choke, cartridge and colour absolutely right? – that they do the inevitable. They miss!

If I am worried about a bird, I know I have only got No 8 cartridges and a fixed-choke gun, so I have to kill the target with those because they are all I have with me. I make sure that all my concentration goes into how I am going to kill the bird and certainly not whether I am

Because I know this bird will be emerging very fast from my left, I have not taken my gun too far back but I am watching for its appearance and will mount quickly as soon as it comes into view.

I will shoot this right to left target right in front of me, but I have turned right back to the trap with the gun as I call for it.

seeing it through the right shade of pink! Keep it simple – there's enough to think about without making it harder for yourself!

I regret that the rule banning the changing of chokes between stands is being relaxed by FITASC from the 1991 season, but I understand there have been problems administering it under the 'new' system. In my opinion, the change will lead to an outbreak of largely unnecessary choke changing.

A New FITASC Layout

Now let us look at a specific new FITASC layout. All the examples shown in this book are based on actual ones shot during the 1990 season in the United Kingdom and in Europe. The ones I have chosen have been selected because they cover a wide variety of targets and are representative of the type of layouts to be found on the competition circuit at home and abroad.

I will start with a 'new' style layout which actually figured in the World championships in France and which was responsible for some very big names falling by the wayside.

Study the diagrams, and you will see how the organisers set out to throw every conceivable type of target on the four shooting layouts, and used speed and angle to great effect. As you will see, the first stand featured a high tower, something that isn't found too often on the Continent and which usually favours British shooters who tend to be more familiar with tower birds.

When you arrive at a stand, always check the targets you are about to shoot. They are usually listed on a card which may look something like this:

Stand One

Singles

Trap 1: Midi, quartering
Trap 2: Normal, quartering
Trap 3: Midi, driven
Trap 4: Normal, driven
Trap 5: Mini, driven

Doubles

Trap 1 and 2, simultaneously

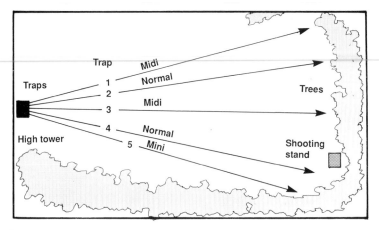

Fig. 1

The first target was a particularly difficult midi, quartering away from the shooting position. The problems it presented were distance and speed and, on top of that, its angle.

Every shooter on my squad failed to connect with the target in the singles and I am certain that we all missed it behind. Because of the considerable speed and distance it was easy to misjudge the required lead. But, more importantly, I think we missed it over the top as well because we failed to 'read' it correctly. It is very easy when shooting this type of target to shoot too high.

Because the bird is quartering away, you tend to forget that it is almost certainly dropping by the time you shoot at it. It appears to be flying true and straight, but because of the angle it isn't possible to see that the bird is actually starting to run out of steam and arcing downwards by the time you get your gun on to it.

It would be far easier to read if it was a straight crossing bird or a high target driven straight towards the shooter. In these particular circumstances, however, the natural reaction is to be concerned with achieving the correct lead – and to forget the flight line.

When a bird comes off a high tower and goes away, it starts to drop when its initial momentum runs out, so if you swing your gun in a straight line you fail to compensate for its downward trajectory. Ideally you should pick up a line *underneath* the bird or shoot it quickly, *before* it starts to drop.

When I shot the target in the doubles, it was one of a simultaneous pair, the other target coming off trap two. The trap two target was almost a straight crosser, quartering away from the shooter only very slightly and didn't require reading nearly as much as the first one.

48

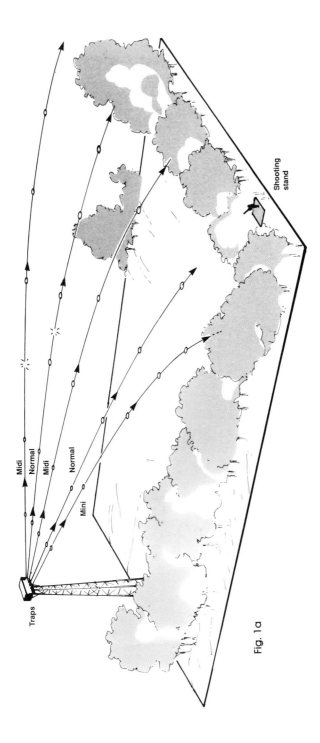

Midi

Normal

Midi

Normal

Mini

Traps

Shooting
stand

Fig. 1a

49

Here's a rare sight – A.J. wearing glasses! I don't like the
glasses or the hat but in this case I was shooting directly
into the sun and had no option.

Kenny Williamson is my regular shooting partner. Here he
displays great concentration as he calls for a target.

In the doubles, I decided to shoot the difficult bird first and, with hindsight, did what I should have done on the singles – I shot it very early, while it was well within range and before it had started dropping. This gave me ample time, having killed it, to swing easily on to the second target of the double and kill that as it passed to my right.

All the other targets on this particular stand, except the one from trap five, were relatively simple driven birds, either to the left or right of the shooting stand. I always use the same technique for tackling driven targets, even if they are not directly overhead as in this case. I bring the gun into my shoulder just under the target and swing through it.

As you will see from Fig 1a, four of the singles were driven, but they were off centre. This was an occasion where the correct footwork was very important. For each target I faced the spot where I expected to kill it and looked back towards the trap as I called for the bird.

You must always decide where you will kill the bird and ensure that your feet are in the correct position, facing the chosen spot. Never make the mistake of facing the trap if it means having to twist your body to shoot the target – your swing will be severely inhibited and the chances are that you will miss.

Watch other people shooting and then decide where you want to kill the target. When you call for the bird, you should be lined up squarely facing the spot you have chosen to kill it. Turn back from your waist in the direction the bird is coming from so you are able to see it as early as possible. This will help you to judge its line correctly so that you can mount and swing through to kill it in the pre-determined place.

Stand Two

```
                 Singles

        Trap 1:  Mini, right-left
        Trap 2:  Midi, right-left
        Trap 3:  Normal, left-right
        Trap 4:  Battue, right-left

                 Doubles

        Trap 2 and 3, simultaneously
```

Stand Two was interesting, if not quite as testing as the previous one. However, one bird did cause me particular difficulty because of its

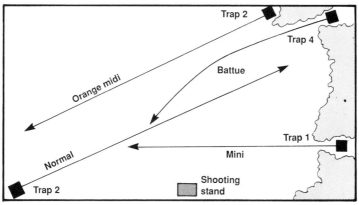

Fig. 2

colour, and that was a fluorescent orange midi off trap two, the only target I missed.

The fluorescent orange target is a serious point of contention with many shooters who have great difficulty judging the speed, and therefore the lead, of this type of target. A few years ago, the International Board of the CPSA banned the use of fluorescent targets in selection shoots and Grand Prix for the ISU disciplines. Trench and skeet shooters had expressed concern about the difficulty in seeing the targets properly.

Some of them, especially the skeet shooters, were unable to judge targets satisfactorily, because their colour produced a fuzzy effect which was primarily evident on crossing birds, and therefore affected the skeet shooters considerably. Many of them complained that they were unable to define the shape of the clay clearly and even experienced the illusion of a comet tail on the bird. Although the International Board banned these targets at home, their use has continued in international competition.

Skeet targets, of course, always fly along a pre-determined trajectory and at quite close range. If skeet shooters have experienced difficulty with fluorescent orange targets, what chance do FITASC shooters have of judging them satisfactorily? We are required to shoot them at far greater distances than skeet targets, and sometimes they are visible for only a very short time, through a gap in trees for instance.

Although there is no doubt that they do show up far more clearly than other colours against certain backgrounds, it doesn't help the person who has difficulty reading their speed and assessing lead. Target visibility could be enhanced by the use of white clays where necessary. I have never heard anyone complain about the difficulty of judging lead when white targets are used. I would like to see fluorescent

I already have this driven target in view and am just about
to bring my gun up to it.

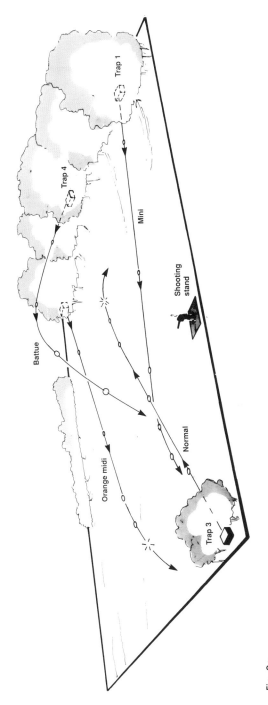

Fig. 2a

55

orange birds banned completely in international competitions, and I think it is time the ISU and FITASC gave the matter serious consideration.

The first target on Stand Two was a mini which emerged from trees and crossed from the right virtually straight in front of the shooter. I killed it straight in front of me, picking it up early, mounting smoothly and swinging through as I squeezed the trigger. It was a simple, straightforward bird which did not pose any unforeseen problems.

As I mount on this high driven target, even my index finger is directly in line with the bird.

I have explained the difficulty I experienced with the fluorescent orange off trap two, the fuzzy image making it virtually impossible for me to judge the correct lead. Much to my irritation for what should have been a relatively easy bird, I missed it in front.

Again, the normal off trap three was a simple quartering target from the left. I turned to my left slightly and shot it as early as possible as it emerged from trees. As I said earlier, you must never let a quartering target go too far or you will miss it in front. In this case, I picked it up quickly and shot its nose with a moving gun. The battue from trap four was high in the air when I killed it, before it started dropping but still giving it plenty of lead.

In the doubles – the normal off trap three and the fluorescent orange – I decided to take no chances with the orange bird. Because I knew I couldn't judge the speed of it, I turned to my left and waited until it had completely run out of steam and rifled it. In other words, I shot straight at it as it started to drop at the end of its flight. I knew that in that position there was no illusion about its position or speed.

The only problem with that was that the simultaneous target off trap three was then far more difficult to kill than if I had shot the flourescent bird early. It had come into view, passed me, then lost its momentum and was dropping quite quickly by the time I got back to it. Luckily, I have full confidence on dropping targets so I was able to get underneath it and kill it.

Ideally, if the first target had not been fluorescent, I would have shot it early and been in a perfect position to pick up the second target with the minimum of movement. If I had shot the first bird early – as I would had it been anything but fluorescent – the second would then have been virtually on the end of my barrels waiting to be killed.

Stand Three

Singles

Trap 1: Normal, quartering left-right
Trap 2: Mini, quartering right-left
Trap 3: Midi, right-left
Trap 4: Teal

Doubles

Trap 2 and 3, simultaneously

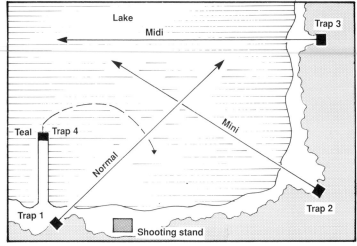

Fig. 3

This layout was one of the most difficult in the competition, with a wide variety of targets, and was an outstanding illustration of the attraction of shooting FITASC Sporting.

Trap one was a normal clay, quartering away across the lake from the shooting position. There was a low, quartering mini off trap two, and from trap three a high, arcing midi. To cap that, trap four threw a very fast teal from the end of a pier about 25 yards away and to the left. There was a catch in every target, no matter how experienced the shooter, and I think it was this layout more than any other which put some of the top performers out of the running.

Let's look at it target by target. First, the normal off trap one. This is a simple enough bird on the face of it, but full of all the potential for disaster inherent in any quartering bird if you leave it too long to shoot it. A quartering target has to be shot as quickly as possible, and in this case I let the bird approach my muzzles and shot it before it had gone too far.

As I explained in my previous book, *Sporting Clays*, quartering targets need very little lead. If you take your gun back to the trap, the likelihood is that you will swing through the bird too quickly and miss it in front. Several people on my squad made that very mistake and I'm sure they were convinced they had missed behind. It is far better to look back for the bird without bringing the gun back as well. Let the target come to the gun before you start swinging. This should prevent you getting too far in front of it.

The second single was a mini off trap two, another quartering target, this time from right to left. I applied exactly the same principles as I had

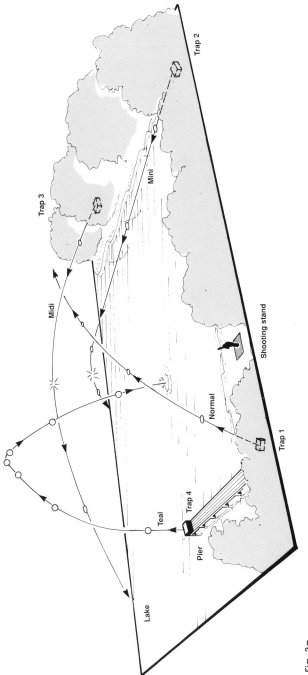

Trap 2

Trap 3

Mini

Midi

Shooting stand

Normal

Trap 1

Teal

Trap 4

Pier

Lake

Fig. 3a

59

Make sure your gun mounting becomes absolutely consistent so you know exactly where the barrels are pointing every time you bring the gun up.

to shoot the first bird, bearing in mind that minis come off the trap very quickly and then slow down much quicker than any other target. In this case I waited for the target to lose its momentum and virtually shot straight at it to kill it.

The target off trap three was a midi, thirty yards out and crossing rapidly from right to left. I decided that the best place to kill this bird was square on as it passed the shooting stand. I set myself up with my feet facing forward and, as the bird was flying quite high, I made sure that I kept the muzzles underneath it as I mounted and pulled through. I killed it exactly where I had planned.

The final single was the springing teal off trap four. In view of its tremendous speed and height, it would probably have been more appropriate to call this bird a screaming teal! From the shooting stand, it was off to the left and thrown from a trap at the end of a pier about twenty-five yards out in the lake. Its trajectory was similar to two sides of a triangle. The bird rose like a rocket, veering away from the vertical to the right before reaching its peak straight in front of the shooter. Then it dropped into the lake to the shooter's right.

You can either shoot teal on the rise or on the way down. I do believe, however, that it is a great mistake to attempt to shoot this type of bird at the peak of its climb as so many people do. In this case, I shot it on the rise, before it reached its peak. In doing this, it is always vital to consider the trajectory of the bird, and this is where many people come unstuck.

There is a subconscious belief that the target is climbing in a straight line and often this is not so. In this case, for instance, to shoot the bird on the rise it was essential to be to the right hand side of it, as I was. The people I saw miss it had assessed the lead correctly, but had not compensated for the target's movement to the right.

They were pulling straight through the bird and squeezing the trigger without 'reading' the flight-line correctly. By the time they fired, the bird had flown off to the right. Other shooters tried to 'rifle' the bird – and by that I mean shoot straight at it – as it reached the top of its climb. I don't agree with this technique as the target is at its peak for only a split second. As soon as the target peaks, it instantly starts to fall. Even if you time it perfectly, and fire at the very moment it 'stops', you will almost certainly miss over the top. In the fraction of a second it takes your pellets to reach it, the target will have started falling fast.

I am certain that the only consistently successful ways to shoot teal are when they are at full speed on the rise or when they are falling. Some people did try to shoot this bird as it was falling, and those I saw miss it did so because they shot below it but again failed to compensate for the fact that the bird was dropping to the right. This target em-

I have just shot an overhead target from behind and am
finishing my downward swing. Note the feet facing directly
ahead for this target.

phasised the need to 'read' the line of a bird before shooting at it. Don't accept what your subconscious tells you, but rather study the target and its trajectory very carefully before you shoot.

The double on this particular stand was quite straightforward: a simultaneous pair, the mini off trap two and the midi off trap three. It should have been simple to shoot the quartering mini and then be in the correct position to pick up the midi coming off trap three. But a momentary lapse of concentration caused me to miss the mini – in front, inevitably – although I did kill the midi.

It is very important to be familiar with the various characteristics of the different types of clays because their individual peculiarities do govern the way you read and shoot them.

Battues, for example, never lose speed like normal clays do. When you see a normal clay face on and dropping, it is usually going slower than when it was under power. A battue, however, whether it is on its edge or flat, *never* loses speed. It maintains the same momentum at every stage of its flight, whether straight or dropping. The tendency for a shooter is always to underestimate its velocity and shoot behind it or over the top because it drops at speed as well.

Don't be fooled by a battue – when you see it dropping and it appears to have slowed down, it is an illusion. Battues need plenty of lead whether in straight flight or when they are falling.

Midis are probably the best target in clay shooting. The midi is especially useful in FITASC, where traps are often placed a long way from the shooter, because it flies truer than any other target. It is also the fastest, and has the combined qualities of the standard and the mini with none of the drawbacks. Because it is slightly heavier than a mini, and lighter than a standard, it will fly a long way at high speed and remain unaffected by wind.

When you go on to a shooting stand, always check the type of target you are shooting. If you are not certain of the type of bird, ask the referee. If you mistake a midi for a normal clay, you will think it is much further away than it is, and the way you approach the bird will be very different.

Minis leave the trap quickly but then slow down twice as quickly as any other target. The worst thing about minis is their tendency to be affected by the wind far more than any other target. Because of their size, it is very easy to misjudge the speed and distance and many shooters are inclined to over-lead them, thinking they are farther away than they actually are.

Rockets fly slower than normal clays and are also much harder to break because, like a rabbit clay, they are very solid. Because they are so thick, it is very rare to see a rocket broken into pieces.

The weight of rockets means that they tend to fly slower than normal clays. As a result, more rockets are missed in front than any other target. A rocket tends to hang in the air so you need to shoot almost straight at it to break it.

Stand Four

Trap 1: Midi, quartering left-right
Trap 2: Midi, crossing left-right
Trap 3: Mini, right-left
Trap 4: Battue, right-left

Doubles

Simultaneous battues from trap 4

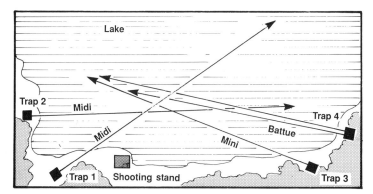

Fig. 4

This was another difficult stand because of the angles and distance of the targets. The midi off trap one was very fast and never gave the shooter a second chance – it had to be shot in the right place the first time or it was gone.

I decided to shoot it as early as possible and coiled my body back towards the trap to pick it up at the first opportunity. I mounted and fired as the bird passed the shooting position. If it had been left any longer, it would have been a very difficult receding edge-on target. By taking it early, I had the fullest possible picture of the clay to shoot at. The midi from trap two was much slower but once again it was fluorescent orange and, almost inevitably, I missed it in front!

Finally, the battue from trap four arced upwards quickly before

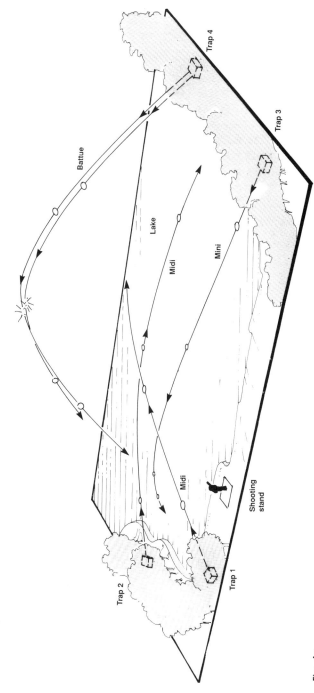

Fig. 4a

starting to fall with equal speed, so I killed it by shooting underneath it just as it started its downward flight.

And on the doubles, I shot both battues in exactly the same spot. After killing the first, I brought my gun back and underneath the second to kill it with carbon-copy precision. I was very careful not to think about the second battue until the first was dead, and I kept my movements unhurried and fluent for the second bird.

Rushing the first target in order to get back for the second is a recipe for missing both birds. Be absolutely clear in your mind what you intend to do and then concentrate completely on the first bird. Kill that before coming back for the second. And remember not to rush it – there is always more time than you think. I finished that particular layout of 25 targets with a score of 21 and, but for the fluorescent orange birds, would have certainly returned a better score.

There is a very fine line between winning and losing at the highest level in FITASC and, out of the top ten international shooters, the one who wins a particular event is the one who kills all the birds he should have. The other nine shooters miss birds they should not have missed and which they are capable of hitting on almost any other occasion. It really is as close as that.

I think that, provided you shoot well and maintain your own standard, you have to be philosophical about defeat. No matter how good you are, there is obviously no possible chance that you will win every time. If I don't shoot a winning score, but at the same time know that I have not done anything completely silly and which has upset me, then I can accept defeat without becoming too disheartened by it.

Once you attain a high standard of shooting, the primary consideration is maintaining that standard and satisfying yourself. If you do that regularly, some days you will win and others you will lose. But you must keep the losses in proportion otherwise your confidence will be affected and your performances will deteriorate. You must accept the fact that no-one on this earth is going to be successful every time.

An Old FITASC Layout

Now I shall describe an 'old' layout, again one I shot during the 1990 season, this time at Anglesey, North Wales, as part of the World Cup Grand Prix series. Water and trees provide a very natural environment for sporting clay shooting, and many FITASC layouts are set up to make the most of natural features such as these. There was a lake at the centre of this particular layout.

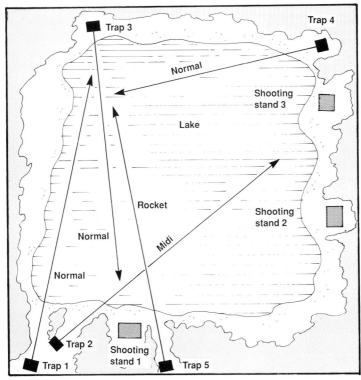

Singles

Trap 1: Normal, left-right
Trap 2: Midi, quartering left-right
Trap 3: Normal, driven
Trap 4: Normal, right-left
Trap 5: Rocket, from behind

Doubles

Simultaneous pair, traps 1 and 3
Pair of battues trap 4, on report

Trap 3

Trap 4

Normal

Shooting
stand 3

Lake

Rocket

Shooting
stand 2

Normal

Midi

Normal

Trap 2

Shooting
stand 1

Trap 1

Trap 5

Fig. 5

The target which most clearly illustrates the point I made earlier about the value of studying a bird on one stand to decide the best place to shoot it later, was the rocket off trap five. On Stand One, it was a straight going-away bird which made it a simple matter to judge its speed

67

This photograph illustrates the high degree of concentration that has to be put into every single target. As you can see, I have eyes only for the target and the furrowed brow emphasises just how hard I am concentrating.

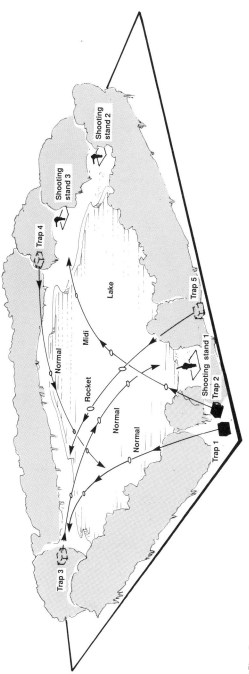

Fig. 5a

accurately. From this position, it was clear that it wasn't going anywhere very quickly at all. If you assess a target in this way, considering the position from which you will be shooting it when you are on later stands, it subsequently becomes much easier to 'read'.

You *should* – and I stress *should* – have an accurate picture of its speed and trajectory, having already experienced it from another angle. But even though they had seen and shot at it before as a going-away target on Stand One, many shooters still misjudged the rocket's speed on Stand Two and shot in front of it. In other words, they had not used their earlier encounter with the target to give them the insight necessary to assist them on subsequent stands.

I honestly don't think shooters use this insight nearly enough. It's the simplest thing in the world, once you have shot a stand and are waiting to move to the next, to consider the targets you have just shot and where they will appear when you are in the new shooting position. In this particular case, I realised on Stand One that we would be shooting the target as a crosser next – and I also noted that it was a rocket which is always a comparatively slow target.

Instead of missing it in front, as many others did on Stand Two, I used my earlier experience of the bird to kill it exactly where I wanted. I *knew* without doubt that the impression of speed was an illusion, and that the target hardly needed any lead at all.

The ability to assess targets in this way is a clear advantage of the 'old' system. There are occasions when you may start off on the first stand with a crossing target, miss it, and feel absolutely sure that you were behind it. Later, however, on a different stand on the same layout, you realise, because the target is now coming straight towards you and therefore easier to judge, how slow it actually is and that you had missed it in front when you shot it earlier. Had you been able to take it as a driven bird first, you would have been in a position to judge its speed far more easily and accurately.

If you look at the diagram and study the trajectory of the clays on different shooting stands, you will see how much the targets change purely because the shooter has moved a few yards into a different position.

For instance, look at the diagram of the layout we are discussing in Fig 5a and you will see that, as well as the Stand One rocket becoming a crosser on Stand Two, there are also considerable changes in the direction of other targets in relation to the shooter. The driven bird off trap three becomes a right-left crosser on Stand Two; the right-left crosser from trap four becomes a going-away bird.

You must take note of all the targets you have the opportunity to study, and as you move round from stand to stand use the knowledge

This high bird is just appearing. Look how my eyes are intently focused on the target as I prepare to bring the gun into my shoulder.

The gun is in my shoulder now and I am about to fire but
my visual contact with the target has never wavered.

you have acquired to make the targets simpler for you to kill. Always use the time when you are not actually shooting to look ahead. Once you get into the habit of doing this, you will find it a tactic of great assistance when you are called to shoot on a new stand.

The target off trap three on this particular layout varied quite considerably from stand to stand but, because I had studied the birds, I was always prepared for the variation.

On Stand One it was coming straight towards me; on Stand Two it was a straightforward crosser; but on Stand Three it became quite technical. From that position the bird was crossing, going slightly away and dropping quite quickly. Some people got the lead exactly right but missed over the top because they hadn't read it properly and allowed for the drop of the bird.

If you concentrate hard and study the birds from stand to stand, you will bring all these variables together in your mind and make allowances for them when you shoot. But if you fail to think ahead, if you don't concentrate and consider the target's trajectory from a different position, you are placing yourself at a serious disadvantage.

Concentrate and think ahead and you will certainly see the benefit reflected on your scorecard.

CHAPTER FOUR

DEMANDING DOUBLES

Now we have had an insight into various FITASC layouts under both systems, let us consider the doubles again.

It really doesn't matter which system you are shooting because, as I have stressed throughout this book, the doubles are undoubtedly your key to success. I cannot emphasise enough how important it is to string doubles together in such a way that the first bird of a pair is killed with the second target in mind. You will be undermining a potentially good score if you kill the first target in the most obvious place but in a spot which makes it virtually impossible to get into the correct place to attack the second.

The golden rule for successfully tackling doubles is *never* to shoot the first bird without having decided exactly where you will shoot the second. I would even go further: the second bird should *always* dictate the precise spot where you will shoot the first.

Ensure that you always prepare as thoroughly as possible for the doubles. If one pair consists of a very difficult bird with an easy one to follow, set yourself up so that, if you do happen to miss the hard one, you can get back into a comfortable position to shoot the second. Although it may sound obvious, don't forget that 50 per cent success is better than nothing and, if you do concentrate too much on that first hard target, the chances are you will miss the easy one too, purely because you are in the wrong position.

If you are shooting the easy bird of a pair first, and are very doubtful about your ability to kill the second, never hesitate to double barrel the first target if you miss it with your first shot. Ignore the second bird and

Never forget to take your gun barrels right back to where you will first pick up the target, ensuring that your feet face the spot where you intend to kill the bird.

shoot for a better percentage. In that way you will build up a competitive score.

As you can imagine, I have shot every conceivable type of double over the years and you may find it helpful if I describe some of them here and explain how to tackle them.

Testing Trench

One pair which sticks in my mind as a former trench shooter, comprised two targets going simultaneously away from the shooter on a trench layout, which in this case was part of one stand in a FITASC competition. This type of target can catch out many sporting shooters but, having shot trench for several years at top level, they do not bother me unduly.

If only one bird is going away and the other is an incomer, you always feel confident that you will kill both birds. The simple reason for this is that one is coming towards you, which means you know you have plenty of time. However, when both birds are heading away as in this case, there is a tendency to rush them. Some people can never get it out of their minds that the targets are receding, and consequently getting harder, every second. Because of this, the instinctive reaction is to rush them – and this is where a lot of people come unstuck. By shooting them too quickly, they miss. In fact, it's highly unlikely that the

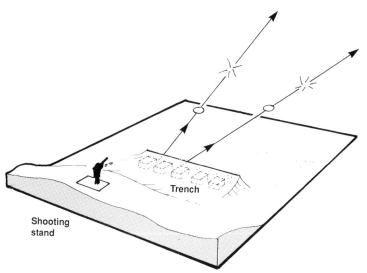

Trench

Shooting
stand

Fig. 6

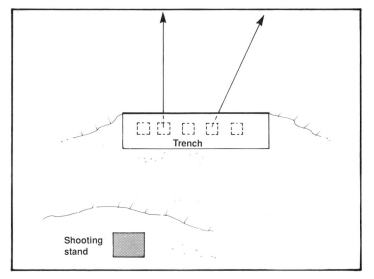

Fig. 6a

birds will ever be out of range, so there really isn't the need to rush that some people imagine. Nevertheless, you must decide which target you are going to shoot first and, having done so, then swing smoothly on to the other.

In this particular case the targets were quite difficult because they were slightly off a straight line and were quartering away. In these circumstances, it is always best to start by shooting the one that is going the straighter. You are able to shoot it quicker because it is fairly straight and that means you have more time to shoot the one that is angled.

I would compare this particular technique with shooting Double Rise. Double Rise is a trap discipline which you shoot from every peg, and on each of them you ensure that you first shoot the bird that is going straight away from you – the one that is going in a straight line. Because you know exactly where it is going, you can be on it half as quickly again as the angled bird, and that gives you time to kill it and then worry about shooting the second one.

When I am coaching, I always teach people to shoot the easier bird of the two first. Because it is straight, it is easy to swing either to the left or right of it and keep the gun flowing for the second bird.

One other important point: if by any chance you miss the first bird, stay on it and give it a second barrel. Remember that, because you are already lined up for it, you have far more time to second barrel it than to swing across and attempt to get in position to shoot the second target.

77

Deceptive Duck, Insidious Incomer

This was a particularly interesting double – a midi quartering towards the shooting stand from about 60 yards away and another thrown simultaneously from behind over the shooter's head. It is a stand which illustrates my constant exhortation to prepare yourself for the second bird before you have even shot the first!

Footwork is absolutely vital in a situation like this. In fact, I placed my feet in the position I wanted them to be to kill the incoming bird, which was quartering across in front of me from right to left. The bird from behind was coming fairly high and rising over my right shoulder. With

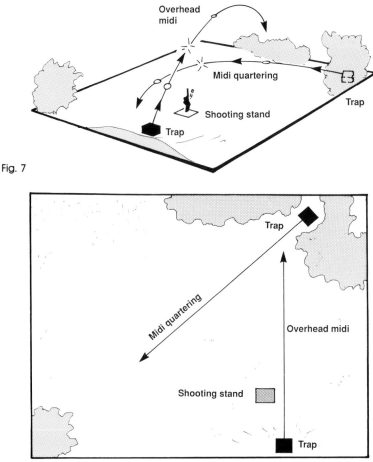

Fig. 7

Fig. 7a

Always make sure that you are totally prepared before you call for the target. Your mind should be clear and you must be concentrating on the target in question and nothing else.

my feet facing the spot where I had decided to kill the incoming bird, I twisted my body to the right and looked back for the overhead target.

I did not give the second bird another thought once I had made up my mind what I was going to do. As I called for the targets, I was looking back for the earliest possible sight of the overhead bird with my gun barrels pointing upwards, ready to swing straight on to it. As soon as the bird came over my head, I shot it and then swung naturally into position for the oncoming target. Because my feet were already facing the point where I had decided to kill it, there was no rush – it was just a very natural body movement.

As my body swung round, there was the incoming midi in the position I had estimated it would be. As a single it was not a difficult bird and, because I prepared for it meticulously, it was just as easy to kill in the doubles.

When facing doubles like this, there is often an inclination for people to fear that the second bird will have gone by the time they have shot the first. If you are not the first to shoot the particular stand, watch carefully and estimate where you think you will be killing the first bird. Then make sure you know where the second one will be at that particular moment. Knowing what you are going to do and how long you have in which to do it, will give you confidence.

I must say that I prefer simultaneous doubles because they are slightly harder than on-report targets, and they make you think a lot more about the way you are going to shoot them. It is essential that you pick the correct bird to shoot first, and that is where we come back to the ability to 'read' targets, and the need to study other shooters if you are not the first on the stand.

With on-report birds, there is only ever one way to shoot them.

Rapid Rabbit, Tortuous Teal

This was a fairly difficult double because, after shooting the rabbit, which was fast and going from right to left, you then had to tackle the teal, fifteen yards in front and to the left of the shooting stand.

I am very confident shooting rabbits. The golden rule is always to point your gun beneath the clay and then consciously to shoot underneath it. If the rabbit has a tendency to bounce, as they often do, you will see it leave the ground and your gun will automatically follow its trajectory. Once it is airborne, it is definitely in the easiest place to shoot because a bouncing rabbit can't go anywhere else!

I can recall this particular double with absolute clarity because I had killed all 23 targets before it on the layout in question. I had already

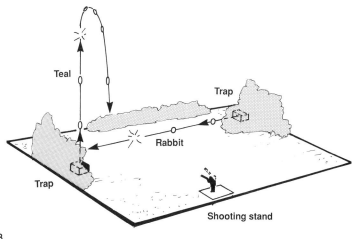

Fig. 8

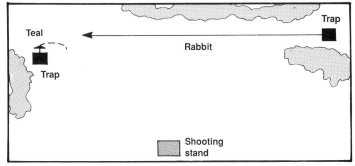

Fig. 8a

convinced myself that I was on for a straight 25 when I called for the targets.

The rabbit was fast, but stayed on the ground and I killed it easily. I was standing with my feet in the correct position for tackling the second target, the teal. It wasn't an easy bird because it was edge-on to the shooter from the moment it left the trap. However, I had killed it with my first barrel in the singles and, until that point, I had done everything absolutely right.

As I swung on to it, however, I inexplicably stopped my gun and did not follow through the flight of the bird. The moment I squeezed the trigger I knew I had missed the target underneath. That unnecessary miss cost me a 25 straight on that particular layout and illustrates the importance of never taking any target for granted.

Although I had killed the rabbit with ease and was perfectly positioned to kill the teal, my concentration lapsed for a fraction of a second. That, and the elementary error of stopping the gun on a moving target, cancelled out all the thorough mental preparation for that particular double – and it ruined my card as well!

Cruel Crosser, Mercurial Mini

These were both tower birds, and the normal which was crossing in front of the shooter from left to right, was flying particularly high and fast about 40 yards out.

The mini was another tower bird, this time from behind and to the right of the shooter. It first came into view over trees slightly behind the stand and then flew very quickly almost over the shooter's right shoulder.

When I watched other competitors shooting this double, it was quite obvious that the mini had to be killed first, and as quickly as possible in order to get on to the crosser, before it disappeared into trees 60 yards away. If I had tried to shoot the pair by taking the crosser first, the mini would have dropped into a position where it was impossible to hit by the time I had swung my gun back to it.

I lined myself up in the position I knew was right to kill the crossing bird from the tower– which was also a helpful stance for the mini coming from behind and to the right. With my feet pointing slightly to the right, I looked back so that I could pick up the bird as soon as possible as it appeared over the trees. As soon as it came into view, I swung my gun in front of it and shot it. Because I did it so quickly, I was then perfectly placed to kill the high crosser off the tower.

It was so fast and so far out that it needed a phenomenal amount

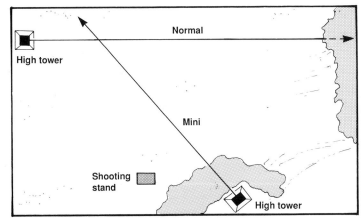

Fig. 9

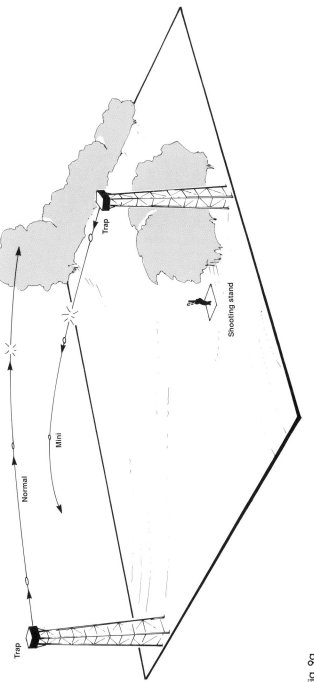

Trap

Normal

Mini

Trap

Shooting stand

Fig. 9a

83

Consistent mounting . . .

... is the secret ...

... of good shooting.

of lead – which I knew from shooting it as a single – so I pulled through it and kept a fast swing going before pulling the trigger. It must have been at least 45 yards out when I killed it and, if I had allowed it to go any further, I may have still been on it but unable to break it.

For any doubters among you, I did kill it quite spectacularly with 28 gram No 8s!

Ruthless Rabbits

This pair of rabbits was visible for only a short time through narrow gaps in trees. One was a straight crosser from right to left, and the other a straight going away target from a trap almost level with the shooter and to his left. It was quite obvious that the crosser had to be killed first, thus leaving the shooter ready to tackle the going-away rabbit. The second target was more difficult than the crosser, because not as much of the bird was visible.

I shot the crosser as it passed the shooting stand, leaving me the

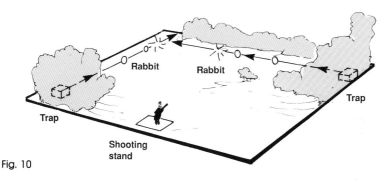

Fig. 10

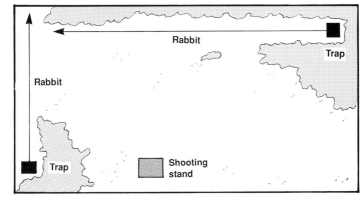

Fig. 10a

87

simple task of just continuing my swing to shoot the going away target. There was absolutely no interruption to the swing, which took the barrels straight into position for the second target.

Whenever possible, keep the swing going in this way so that it will naturally take you on to the second target of a pair. If you do this, the movement will always be far more fluent than if you check and then start to swing again. There is always a danger if you do check your swing, that the second target will be gone by the time you resume your movement and bring the gun into the right position. Certainly if I had checked before moving on to the second target in this particular case, the rabbit would not have been visible.

When you are shooting doubles on a stand where it is not obvious to you which bird you should take first, or where you are unable to make up your mind, make sure you watch other people shooting. If you are unfortunate enough to be the first shooter in such circumstances, it is vital that you make a decision and are completely clear in your own mind which target you are going to shoot first.

We have all watched someone call for a pair of targets when he is not certain which bird to take first. Then you have the crazy situation where he brings up his gun and shoots in between the two birds because he has still not made a decision. This always results in the loss of the pair.

I always take great care to be absolutely certain what I am going to do when I do go on to a stand. For instance, I have stood on a shooting stand facing a teal which rose up very steeply in front of me and then went over my head and dropped behind. I could have murdered it as it went up, but the second part of the double was a driven pheasant. Instead of shooting the teal on the rise, I waited and killed it as it arced over and, in doing so, I was in an ideal place to kill the pheasant with the minimum amount of gun movement.

If you are to accumulate a challenging score, every double must be thought out like that. *Never* go on a stand in two minds because, if you do, you will almost certainly miss both targets. It's far better to go for just one bird with both barrels than miss them both through indecision.

And don't be intimidated by the doubles. As I hope I have illustrated, by giving them some serious thought while you are waiting to shoot, and by watching other more experienced shooters, you will soon discover that there is a straightforward way to shoot most of them.

I am certainly not suggesting that by carefully thinking them through you will never have a problem with a simultaneous pair again. What you will find, though, is that birds which appear very difficult at first sight can be simplified considerably with concentration and a little logical and constructive thought.

A.J. – always under intense presssure.

Always prepared to give total concentration to every bird – one miss can mean the difference between success and failure.

You will never record a satisfying score at FITASC until you get to grips with doubles on a regular basis. Take my word for it – if you can hit most birds as singles, there is absolutely no reason why you shouldn't be able to cope with them as doubles.

Shooting FITASC seriously means a protracted learning curve and a serious will to succeed. It demands natural talent and the utmost dedication to reach the top. It necessitates regular practice and a desire to compete as often as possible. And it also requires the capacity not to be disheartened by setbacks, the disappointing performances which are certain to occur.

FITASC is expensive and at the highest level requires the type of dedication which is common in any sport. There are, however, some relatively simple exercises which can make the transition from beginner to combative performer a slightly quicker process and I shall summarise them here. I have already covered most of them in preceding chapters, but you may find it helpful to have a checklist of the various tactics you can employ to help to improve your scores.

The Golden Rules

* If you are really serious about competitive shooting – and by that I mean at national level and not just at the local Sunday morning event – you *must* master doubles before you can hope to be really competitive.

The more proficient you become, the more your confidence will grow and with it an unshakeable belief in your own ability. Once you have achieved the confidence to match the proficiency of your shooting, you will be well on your way to success.

* Be prepared, too, to visit a reputable coach if you are experiencing a persistent problem with your shooting. A difficulty which may cause you heartache for months – and lose you many valuable birds into the bargain – can often be overcome quite simply.

A good coach is invaluable, so never think that you know it all, and don't be too proud to seek assistance. Even a slight adjustment to your stance or the way you mount, perhaps even a minor alteration to the fit of your gun, could make an enormous difference to the accuracy and efficiency of your shooting.

* Remember that there are no short-cuts to success. There is no easy or magical substitute for hard work, regular competition and a willingness to learn from every adverse situation. In the preceding chapters I have described the most obvious and simple ways to shoot a wide variety of targets. Simplicity is the key to most successful shooting so always bear in mind the following important points.

Make sure that you study the targets carefully before you shoot them and that you have made up your mind exactly what you are going to do.

* Use the gun and cartridge combination that suits you and cut down on extraneous diversions like assorted tints for your glasses.
* When you have decided which way to stand for a particular target, always turn to look for the bird so that you are able to see it as soon as possible when it leaves the trap. The earlier you see the target, the easier it is to judge its line of flight.
* When you are shooting, ignore the people behind you who are waiting their turn and never allow their presence to panic you into doing something you never intended.
* In the same situation, don't ever be intimidated. We all have to learn and you will not perform to the best of your ability if you are worrying about what other people are thinking.
* If you have the slightest doubt about the type of target you are about to shoot – whether it is a normal or a midi, for instance – check the card or ask the referee to clarify it.
* Study the way in which other shooters – especially those with a reputation for good shooting – tackle different targets. You can learn a lot watching a champion in action on different types of bird.

* Learn to concentrate at will. Remember that a FITASC squad can finish shooting one layout and then be waiting for a considerable time before shooting another.

You must be able to switch your concentration on again the moment you are back on a layout, despite having just relaxed in the club-house for a couple of hours. This ability to close the mind to everything but the targets comes with practice and is a quality shared by all the best shooters.

* If you are fortunate enough to be able to travel abroad, then go and sample the excellent layouts in Europe, and especially in France, the spiritual home of FITASC.

* Never underestimate the 'new' system, because there is no doubt that it's here to stay. There are some shooters who will use any opportunity to criticise it but, when it is run well on a ground with plenty of space, it is just as exciting and challenging as traditional FITASC.

* If you already shoot a discipline such as skeet or trap, use your experience and technique to help your sporting shooting. There are so many going-away and crossing targets in FITASC, that knowledge and experience of a discipline can be of great benefit.

* Never be afraid to seek advice from other shooters, especially the experienced ones. Most will be only too happy to help and their knowledge and insight will be invaluable.

CHAPTER FIVE

A FLOURISHING FUTURE?

Clay shooting is more popular today than at any time in its 100-year history and there are tangible indications that interest in FITASC, too, is growing worldwide. Shooters from every European country, and even from as far away as Australia and New Zealand, participate in major competitions all over the world now as a matter of course.

I have not the slightest doubt, however, that the country that will influence the development of FITASC more than any other is the United States. Since the Americans first started shooting English Sporting in 1985, its progress and development in the USA have been little short of phenomenal. As I pointed out in Chapter One, American shooters have long been associated with outstanding clay shooting in the Olympic disciplines, and their facilities for trap and skeet are among the finest in the world. But the speed with which sporting has grown in the USA since the mid-1980s has been breathtakng.

In 1985 there were only two courses specifically designed for sporting clays, both of them at Houston in Texas. By the end of 1990 there were an astonishing 200 sporting layouts nationwide, and the facilities at most of them would make the average British club shooter green with envy.

The problems which plague clay shooting in the United Kingdom and inhibit financial investment in the sport – strict planning controls and the new and more stringent firearms legislation – are virtually unknown in America. When the owners of clubs invest large sums of money to provide shooters and their families with the finest facilities, they do so secure in the knowledge that they can expect a long-term return on their outlay. In the UK, we are all aware how easy it is for shooting

Concentrate solely on the job in hand – killing the next target. And don't let the presence of spectators worry you. Their attention is inevitable in a big championship event.

grounds to have their activities severely curtailed or shut down completely by local authorities, especially if there are complaints about noise. Some of our best known and best run shooting grounds have run into problems recently, even though they have operated satisfactorily for many years. It is understandable, therefore, that many ground owners are cautious when they consider investment in ground facilities not directly connected with the actual shooting, such as a new club-house, for instance.

In America, where grounds do not face the constant threat of suddenly being forced out of business, the financial investment has been enormous in the last couple of years and the resulting facilities are very impressive.

'Golf with a Shotgun'

I believe much of the success and growth of sporting clay shooting in America is a result of the hard work of the United States Sporting Clays

Targets such as these which are quite a way out will probably require a considerable amount of lead, so be sure to swing right through them from behind as smoothly as possible.

Association. It was Bob Davis, the association's president and chairman, who dreamed up the catchy slogan which described sporting clay shooting as 'golf with a shotgun'.

The phrase caught the imagination of the American media and the public, and it not only attracted considerable publicity but also played a large part in attracting a whole new set of shooters to attempt sporting clay shooting. It is not uncommon now to see shooters on American layouts using electrically-operated golf trolleys to move from stand to stand! I would be delighted if clay shooting in the UK could attract the type of positive publicity and investment that it does in the United States and also throughout most of Europe.

The Flint Oak Gun Club at Fall River, Kansas, is typical of many of the new, superbly-appointed sporting clay clubs which have opened in the United States on the crest of the sporting wave.

Half a million dollars have been invested there. All the traps are electrically and computer controlled and the shooting stands have been built in elevated positions overlooking a lake – 'TV and spectator ready' according to the club's owner. That sort of confidence reflects tremendous belief in the sport's future and has generated considerable public and media interest in clay shooting all over the US.

Now that Americans have been shooting English Sporting for five years, they are determined to become successful at FITASC. They emphasised that determination by winning three bronze medals at the 1990 World championships in France. I happen to know that America is already hoping to stage one of the major FITASC championships in the very near future. Surely the fact that so many British and mainland European shooters were prepared to cross the Atlantic to take part in the US national championships in 1990 augurs well for the support that a big international FITASC event, such as the World championship, would command if it was held in America.

I am convinced, however, that American shooters will be successful at international level in both team and international events in the next few seasons, and there are very real signs that the French, too, are re-emerging as a power to be reckoned with once again. It may be that the British dominance of FITASC could really be under threat at last.

In Europe, successful shooters are household names, as popular and as well known as soccer stars are in Great Britain or baseball stars in the USA. An illustration of this is that, when the excellent trap shooter, John Grice, won his World Universal Trench championship in 1990, he was astonished to find himself the toast of the town at Lonato in Italy, where the championships were staged. He was even asked for his autograph by Italians who recognised him in the street after watching his gold medal victory live on television. I gather the instant celebrity status came as something of a surprise to John. That sort of thing doesn't happen too often in rural Staffordshire where he lives!

In America and Europe there is genuine public interest in clay shooting. Perhaps if the sport was televised in the UK, it would help to 'sell' shooting to a wider audience and so attract more commercial investment. It would certainly be nice to think so.

New Names for Gold?

If you check the details of previous winners of World and European titles at the back of this book, you will observe that the French record at FITASC shooting was consistently successful until 1984. Since then, however, they have won the World title only once – in 1986, when Pascal Delaroche was the victor.

I have won it twice and John Bidwell and Mickey Rouse have also been victorious since, although Mickey's brilliant victory in 1990 was something of a face-saver as the French took the other leading places as well as the team event.

All the signs are that the French have the bit between their teeth again and are regularly shooting much harder targets at home than they were previously. They seem to have rediscovered their competitive edge. The targets and layouts they organised for the 1990 World championships at Le Rabot were outstanding. I do find it quite astonishing, though, that even on the Continent, where FITASC is shot constantly because there is no English Sporting, the discipline is still dominated as it is here by shooters who were at the top at least a decade ago.

Legendary performers, like France's Michel Riboulet and the ever-green Marc Polet, from Belgium, are still at the top and setting a blistering pace all these years on. It seems that in Europe, as in the United Kingdom, they are still waiting for that new generation of world-class shooters to break through and start challenging for the top honours. Because of the concentration on FITASC in Europe, I would really have expected the new blood to have come through and been pressing for major titles already.

In the meantime, I think that, if the number of shooters wishing to participate in major championships continues to increase on the scale of recent years, then the administrators of FITASC will be faced with another very real problem induced by the discipline's popularity.

FITASC, as we know, has a clearly stated policy of staging 'open' competitions which enable all clay shooters to compete in major competitions without having to qualify, which, as I pointed out earlier, is the case in the ISU-controlled disciplines. There were more than 700

The strain of waiting to shoot in a big competition can
manifest itself in many ways!

shooters in the 1990 World championships and all the indications are that there will be even more entrants in future seasons.

Will the growth force FITASC into a situation where they have to introduce a selection procedure whereby shooters must qualify to participate in the major competitions? It would be a great pity if that did happen, but how many entries can be accepted before an event becomes so unwieldy as to be virtually impossible to stage satisfactorily?

I don't envy FITASC the problem, but deep down I have a sneaking feeling that they will remain true to their belief that FITASC events should be open to any individual who wishes to participate. I sincerely hope so.

Show Some Pride

Although we win more international medals for shooting than in any other sport, it is astonishing to consider that Great Britain has only once won an Olympic gold medal. That was more than 20 years ago in 1968 when Bob Braithwaite, a vet from Lancaster, won the Olympic Trap event in Mexico City.

I suspect that the only reason we have not done as well at trap and skeet as we have at sporting, is that our shooters don't have adequate facilities for training in the Olympic disciplines. Setting up regulation Olympic Trap, with fifteen traps for each layout, is a very expensive business and the number of satisfactory grounds in the UK can be counted on the fingers of one hand. Consequently, our trap inter-nationals usually have to travel considerable distances to practise.

It certainly isn't a lack of shooting ability that keeps us out of the Olympic medals table and we prove that time and again with our success in other disciplines.

We sporting shooters are very fortunate to be able to shoot excellent targets week in and week out and I would like to see our colleagues in the ISU disciplines with better facilities. Once again, the answer lies in the size of the financial investment the sport is able to to attract.

I do happen to believe that shooting could attract more outside finance if some grass-roots competitors did more to improve the image of the sport by looking the part and dressing better when they attend shoots. I regret to say that the way some people turn themselves out is a disgrace and doesn't do anything to enhance the sport's image in the eyes of outsiders, and that includes potential sponsors.

Shooting is not cheap. The initial outlay for a gun is certain to be at least several hundred pounds and, on top of that, there is the regular purchase of cartridges. Is it too expensive, then, to buy a decent skeet vest? Check the range marketed by that great supporter of clay

Use the time when you are waiting to shoot to your best
advantage by studying the way the shooter in front of you
tackles a particular bird.

Here, I'm watching for the bird and preparing to mount the gun. Some shooters tend to grip the gun's fore-end far too tightly, and in this picture you can see how relaxed my grip is. Because I am left-handed, my right hand is used to push the gun barrels in front of the target and a relaxed hold makes for a much more fluent swing.

shooting, Laurie Armistead of Ganton, and you will see what I mean. They are available right across the price range, and in a multitide of colours, so there is absolutely no excuse for turning up at your shoot looking scruffy.

Golfers always manage to look smart, and so do the personalities in popular televised sport, such as snooker. Snooker now has a code of conduct for dress and I think the players' appearance is a credit to them. Being smart can work wonders in giving an impression of responsibility, so think carefully about the way you look the next time you are setting off to a shoot.

Consider Others

Always bear in mind the inconvenience you may be causing to non-shooters through noise. There are excellent shooting grounds all over the UK which have been deliberately situated well away from people's homes and where no-one is disturbed by 150 people shooting 100 targets each on a Sunday morning.

Unfortunately, the popularity of clay shooting has spawned another breed of ground owner interested only in getting people through the stands with little or no regard for the inconvenience that may be caused to others.

I have been shooting for as long as I can remember but I don't think even I would want a clay shooting ground at the bottom of my garden. But there are now grounds which have actually opened up well within earshot of houses and don't hesitate to start their Sunday morning events at 9 a.m. – without the slightest regard for the people living nearby. That is obviously not good enough and, if you care about your sport and its ability to co-exist with others, boycott the grounds which clearly don't care.

Because we love shooting, none of us must shirk our responsibilities. We must be prepared to act in unison, or individually if necessary, to put a stop to anything which may jeopardise clay shooting's future.

Mobile Layouts

When I first started shooting FITASC, there is no doubt that, as far as the quality of grounds and targets was concerned, Portugal led the way. At Vilamoura and Lisbon, the Portuguese showed great foresight by installing the latest automatic traps and towers and, until about 1986, they were able to throw the finest targets of all.

Another example of the relaxed hand hold on the fore-end. You can also see here that my left hand is not holding the stock too tightly either.

Here I have called for the target and am still waiting for it to appear. To my right is the card you will find on all FITASC stands which details the targets, singles and doubles, to be shot from a particular stand.

Recently, however, the whole method of staging FITASC championships has changed dramatically. The discipline has suddenly become completely 'mobile'. Shoot organisers are no longer restricted to staging competitions on established shooting grounds. Companies like Laporte, who manufacture traps and clays, are now willing to take their superb range of traps anywhere in the world and set up a shoot wherever it is required.

For instance, in 1989 the World championships were staged at Vilars-sur-Olion in the Swiss Alps amid beautiful surroundings and scenery with breathtaking snow-capped peaks all around. Every single piece of equipment necessary for that shoot, including all the traps, was taken up the mountain to create a shooting ground on absolutely virgin mountainside. All the officials and shooters had to use a cable-car to reach the layouts, and the targets were outstanding, a credit to the foresight of the organisers.

Theirs was a visionary move. Now we are no longer restricted to established grounds, and that obviously means that the potential for developing new and even more challenging 'one-off' layouts is endless.

There is also one other advantage which I believe makes a shoot staged in these circumstances equally fair for every single competitor. Because the layout is set up for only one specific event, the 'home' shooters are unable to practise on the targets before the officially-designated practice days shortly before the competition.

Professional Referees

As FITASC has become more organised and competitive, it has also been noticeable how much more professional the referees have become.

In the early days, people refereed purely for the money but now there are more professional people refereeing. Many of them are people who love shooting but are not good enough to compete at the highest level. To stay involved in major competitions, they become referees and, in my opinion, the standard of refereeing has become more professional and consistent.

I am not in any way being critical of the people who used to be referees, but the new influx of professional people – many of whom are used to having authority in their working lives – has resulted in a much higher standard. Shooting in general has become more competitive and professional. Surely it follows that refereeing should be equally professional.

The final few targets on the last layout in a big FITASC
competition always attract an audience. Take no notice
of them and ensure that you concentrate on the job in
hand – killing the next target.

There is much that is good happening in clay shooting today, and
despite the continuing problems facing the sport in general, I remain
very optimistic for the future. All of us who shoot clays are fortunate to
be part of such a friendly and competitive worldwide sporting movement. It is the responsibility of every single one of us to ensure that the
very special camaraderie of clay shooting is preserved and nurtured.

In that way we will all continue to enjoy it at every level, from the
smallest 'straw bale' village shoot to the most fiercely-contested World
championship. Don't rely on others to promote your sport for you – we
must all be ambassadors for clay shooting every time we attend an
event, no matter how small it may be.

And, if reading this book helps you to kill just one extra target when
you next shoot FITASC, I shall consider that it has succeeded.

CHAPTER SIX

RULES AND REGULATIONS

The following are the rules and regulations for International (FITASC) Sporting. They are reproduced by kind permission of the Clay Pigeon Shooting Association. Imminent amendments to the rules on gun mounting and choke changing are covered in the main text.

Shooting Stand

Article 1 Following the configuration of the grounds, a sporting layout must be equipped with a sufficient number of traps so that the competitors wil shoot under conditions as close as possible to game shooting – partridges, pheasant, ducks, rabbits, in front, low, high, crossing and quartering, in fields or in woods, hidden or not by trees and bushes.

The ground must have been approved by the national Federation for the organisation of the national competitions and by the international Federation for the organisation of the international competitions.

Clays

Article 2 The clays to be used are the regular trench, skeet and rabbit-shooting clays, thinner clays and clays with a smaller diameter which have a higher speed, and possibly electric targets.

Shooting Position

Article 3 The shooter will adopt the standing position, his feet within the limits of the shooting stand, his gun held with two hands clearly out of the shoulder, gun touching the body under the armpit. He will keep this position until the bird or birds are in sight.

The departure of the birds is given by the referee after the shooter has pronounced the word 'Ready' (Prêt).

If the marksman positions himself wrongly or shoulders his gun before the target appears, he will receive a warning. A second fault will cause a 'No Bird' and if there is a third fault in the same run (sequence) a 'Nought' (Zero) will be called or, in the case of a double, a 'Zero, Zero'.

The shooter has no right to refuse the bird unless he has not pronounced the word 'Ready'.

Shooting posts will be marked by squares of 0.91m on one side or circles of 1m diameter.

When the bird is in sight, the shooter must shoulder his gun in order to fire at all the clays, even the rabbits.

Trajectories

Article 4 For the championships or international championships, a Sporting Committee will be formed which will be entrusted with the task of fixing, at the latest the day before the competition, the different trajectories of the clays which will be shot during the event. No training will be permitted before the events take place on the course or courses (parcours) fixed by the Technical Committee.

At each stand, the setting of the trajectories for all the shooters must be strictly the same in height, distance and speed.

Before the championship, the shoot organiser will establish a plan showing the trajectories of the traps. These trajectories, established and calculated in calm weather, may be altered by wind.

Irregular Birds

Article 5 The following are considered as irregular birds:

– two birds launched at the same time for a single.
– birds broken on leaving the trap. Under no circumstances will the result of shooting a no-bird be counted.

Irregular Doubles

a) When either or both birds in a double are irregular

b)If only one bird is launched in a double. After a judge has declared a 'No Bird', firing cannot continue. After a warning, the marksman will receive a zero penalty.

Organisation of Competitions

Article 6 Shooting will be in squads of a maximum of six shooters. If necessary, it is permissible to form squads of at least three shooters.

The organising committee in agreement with the jury can fill vacancies by non-competitive shooters who will shoot for 'birds only'.

Article 7 During international competitions the shooters of each country shall be dispersed over the various squads. The organising committee will announce the arrangements for a draw at a previously determined hour so that national delegates can be present.

If, during the draw for the shooting squads, members of a family find themselves in the same group, they will be able, before the competition begins, to ask the organising committee to regroup them in different squads of shooters.

Article 8 Shooting takes place in squads of six shooters as drawn, with moving up of the shooter not only at each stand but also for shooting doubles when certain stands call for the shooting of doubles.

At each stand the shooters of a squad will first fire at the single birds and, if necessary, the six shooters will then fire at the doubles.

e.g. Stand 1 – A single, shooting in the following order: 1 2 3 4 5 6.
Stand 1 – Doubles, in the following order: 2 3 4 5 6 1.
Stand 2 – Singles, in the following order: 3 4 5 6 1 2.
Stand 2 – Doubles, in the following order: 4 5 6 1 2 3.

All the targets will be exhibited once at post 1 and subsequently only new targets will be shown. The shooters are not allowed to fire or swing their guns at the birds.

Article 9 Shooting occurs in sequences of 25 or 30 birds, singles, simultaneous doubles, doubles 'on the gun' in which the second bird is thrown only when a shot has been fired at the first target.

However, the referee can, in exceptional circumstances, interrupt shooting if there is sudden heavy rainfall or a storm which seems to be of short duration.

Article 10 If one of the shooters is not present when his name is called, the referee must call his name and number loudly three times for a period of one minute. If the shooter does not then appear, shooting will start without him.

Once the first bird of this series is shot, a late arriving shooter can only take his place in the group if the first shooter of the group has not yet taken up his position to shoot his second bird.

During a championship, any shooter who does not answer when his name is called will be allowed to shoot in another squad but his first three killed birds will be scored zero.

Article 11 In the case of a malfunction of a trap during the shoot, the referee will decide if the round must be continued on another stand or on the same one after the mechanical trouble has been rectified. The squad has the right to see another bird before starting again.

Article 12 During international competitions, the scores will be kept by three persons.

Immediately after each series, the scores are compared and the possible differences resolved for each bird. The scores of each series are then posted on a central notice board.

Article 13 On the course (parcours) chosen by the Technical Committee (see *Article 19a*) it will not be possible to shoot targets in training.

Referees and Jury

Article 14 Shooting will be supervised by a referee who normally has to be in possession of a referee's certificate and has clay-shooting experience. His principal role consists of deciding, after each bird is thrown, whether the bird is killed or not and clearly signify if it has been lost or was irregular.

Article 15 The referee will be assisted by two auxiliaries and a marker whom he will have chosen from the preceding squad. Shooters are not allowed to refuse to do this job, but the referee can accept a substitute.

The principal function of the auxiliary referees is to record on a score sheet the results which they ascertain.

The marker has to record on a score sheet the results announced by the referee.

Article 16 The referee has to decide immediately if a new bird must be launched following a technical difficulty or for any other reason. He has to say 'No Bird' if possible before the shooter fires his first shot.

Article 17 The principal referee takes all the decisions alone. If one of the auxiliary referees holds another opinion, he should raise his arm to inform the principal referee who will then make a definitive decision.

Jury

Article 18 International events will be supervised by a jury consisting of a representative of each country participating, with the representative of the organising country as chairman.

The jury makes decisions by a majority vote. In the case of equal votes, the chairman's vote is final. The jury can make valid decisions when the chairman and two members are present.

In urgent cases, two members who are unanimous over a decision can, by way of exception, make it in consultation with the referee.

Article 19 The role of the Jury is:

a) To appoint a Technical Committee in order to fix, on the day before the competition, the various trajectories, the location of the shooting stands, the choice and speed of the targets which will be shot during the event.
b) To verify before shooting begins that the range conforms to regulations and that the preparatory arrangements are suitable and correct.
c) To see that during shooting the rules are adhered to and to inspect the weapons, ammunition and targets by means of test or otherwise.
d) To make the necessary decisions in cases of technical defects or other disturbances during shooting if these are not resolved by the referee.
e) To deal with protests.
f) To make decisions regarding penalties when it concerns a shooter who does not adhere to the rules or behaves in an unsportsmanlike manner.
g) To make sure that there are always at least two members of the jury present at the shooting ground.

Article 20 The decisions of the jury cannot be appealed against unless a special appeal jury has been appointed for the competition.

Weapons and Ammunition

All weapons, including automatics, are allowed providing their calibre does not exceed 12 bore. No handicap will be given to shooters using guns of a calibre smaller than 12.

Any changing of weapon (or any part of the weapon which functions normally, adjustable chokes included) is forbidden throughout the duration of the competition.

Any infringement of this rule will automatically lead to the disqualification of the competitor.

Article 22 The load of the cartridge may not exceed 36 grams of shot. The shot will be spherical and of solid lead, diameter between 2 and 2.5mm.

Cartridges must be normally loaded.

The use of dispersers or dispersion devices or abnormal loading of cartridges (including reversed loading) is forbidden.

The referee can, at any moment, take an unfired cartridge out of the shooter's gun for examination. The use of black powder is forbidden, as is the use of tracer cartridges.

Article 23 In case of jamming of the gun, which on the referee's decision cannot be repaired on the spot, without being the shooter's fault, the latter will be allowed to fire with another gun if he can get one immediately.

Otherwise, he will have to leave his place and round and will shoot his remaining birds in another round where there is room, with the referee's permission.

If the gun is repaired before the round is finished by his squad, the shooter can take his place on the squad, again with the referee's permission.

In case of other malfunction of the gun or the cartridges, resulting in inability to fire, and without it being the shooter's fault, the latter may choose to change guns or continue with the same.

He will have the right to another bird three times during the same round of 25 birds in all the cases of malfunction proscribed in the rules, without taking into consideration whether he has changed his gun or not.

The fourth malfunction and the following will be scored as zero.

Article 24 Two cartridges can be used on each single bird, but the shooter will only be allowed two cartridges for each double.

In the doubles, the shooter has the right to shoot either of the two birds first.

In a double, if the two birds are killed with one shot, they will be scored 'killed – killed'.

113

In a double, the shooter, having missed the first bird, may fire his second cartridge at the same bird.

When shooting a double 'on the gun', the shooter will have the right, if he misses the first bird, to fire his second shot at the same bird, the result being counted on the first bird, the second bird being counted zero.

Article 25 When a shooter is ready to fire, he announces 'ready' to the trapper, and the bird must be launched within the time of 0 to 3 seconds.

When the shooter has announced 'ready', he has to stick to the position described in *Article 3* until the bird is in sight.

Killed or Missed Birds

Article 26 The bird is killed when it has been launched and the shooter has shot it according to the rules, and at least one visible bit of it has broken off or it has been totally or partly pulverised.

Article 27 The bird is missed:

a) When it has not been hit.
b) If only dust goes off (smoked or deflected bird).
c) If the shooter is unable to fire because he left the safety catch on, has forgotten to load or cock, if the gun has not been sufficiently broken or closed or if the shooter has forgotten to take the necessary measures to load the cartridge chamber (when he uses a single barrel gun).
d) If it is the fourth or more malfunction of the gun or ammunition occurring in the same round of 25 birds.
e) If the shooter is unable to fire his second shot, having put in a second cartridge or if he has not cancelled the locking device of the loading chamber in an automatic weapon, or if the safety catch engages due to the recoil of the first shot, or if the second cartridge is ejected by the recoil or opened and emptied due to the recoil, or for any other reason.
f) If the second shot cannot be fired because a shooter using a single trigger gun has not released it sufficiently after having fired his first shot.
g) If the shooter, in case of malfunction, opens it himself or touches the safety catch before the referee has examined the gun.
h) If the shot is not fired for another reason which does not give right to another bird.

i) If the shooter adopts a waiting position which is not according to *Article 3* and if he has been warned once during the same round.

New Clay – 'No Bird'

Article 28 The clay will be 'No Bird' and a new target will be launched, the shooter having fired or not:

a) If the bird is broken at the start.
b) If the bird is launched from the wrong trap.
c) If two birds are launched simultaneously when a single should have been thrown.
d) If the bird is definitely of another colour than the birds used for the competition.
e) If the first bird of a double is regular and the second irregular, or conversely.
f) If two birds are launched simultaneously during a double 'on the gun'.

Article 29 The bird will be delcared 'No Bird' and a new bird will be launched, the shooter *not* having fired:

a) If the bird is launched before the shooter has said 'ready'.
b) If the bird is launched after a delay of more than 3 seconds.
c) If the bird zigzags, if its initial speed is not sufficient or if its trajectory is irregular.
d) If the shooter is not in the waiting or shooting position proscribed by the rules (first warning).

   No complaint of irregularity will be accepted when, in singles as well as doubles, the bird or birds have been shot at, if the irregularity in question consists simply of either a normal deviation of the trajectory of the bird or of a premature or delayed release, unless the referee has distinctly called 'No Bird' before the shooter has fired in the case of a premature release, or before the appearance of the bird in the case of a delayed release.

   In all other cases, the result will be counted when a shooter has fired.

Article 30 In case of misfiring of the cartridge or a malfunction of the gun not attributable to the shooter, the bird will be declared 'No Bird' and a new bird will be launched; after three misfires or malfunctions in the same round of 25 birds (the shooter having exchanged guns or not) further incidents will be scored as lost.

Article 31 The referee may also order the launching of a new bird when:

a) The shooter has been cleary disturbed.
b) Another competitor fires at the same target.
c) The referee for any reason cannot decide if the bird has been killed or lost. The referee must also consult his assistants before allowing a new bird under this rule.

The referee cannot in any case give a 'No Bird' if the shooter has missed for any other reason than the ones stated in the 'No Bird' rules.

Article 32 The rules of *Articles 23* to *28* apply equally to the firing of doubles, simultaneous doubles and rafale doubles and will be interpreted as follows:

a) The double will be declared 'No Bird' and the shooter will be asked to fire a second double to determine the scores of the two shots if:
   1. The first bird is regular and the second irregular, without taking into account whether the first one is killed or not.
   2. A malfunction of the gun or sartorial prevents the shooter from shooting his first bird.
   3. One or the other bird from a double is irregular and the shooter does not fire. If the irregularity in question is a deviation from the normal trajectory, an insufficient speed or a too quick or too slow launching and the two birds have been shot at, the results must be counted.
   4. The first bird is regular and has been shot at, but the second bird is late or does not leave the trap.
      If the shooter misses his first bird and this collides with the second before the shooter has fired his second shot; if the fragments of the first bird break the second before the shooter has fired his second shot.
   5. The referee denies the right of the shooter to fire his second shot because of the violation of *Article 3* provided that the shooter has not been warned for the same reason during the same round; otherwise the result of the first shot will be scored and the second bird declared lost.
   6. If in a double the first bird is missed and the second shot cannot be fired because of malfunction of the gun or ammunition.
b) The bird will be declared 'lost':
   1. On the fourth malfunction of the gun or misfiring of the cartridge in the same round.
   2. If the shooter (without legitimate reason) does not shoot a regular double.
   3. If the shooter (without legitimate reason) does not shoot the

116

second bird of a regular double, the result of the first bird is scored and the second will be declared lost.

Article 33 If during a double the gun fires both shots simultaneously, the double will be declared 'No Bird' and be shot again, even if the first bird has been killed.

Article 34 A shot will be considered as not fired:

a) If the shooter fires although it is not his turn to fire.
b) If the shooter involuntarily fires a shot on his turn, but before having given the signal.

Article 35 When shooting doubles 'on the gun' the following will be awarded:

a) Kill and zero if the shooter breaks the first bird and misses the second.
b) Kill and no bird, the double having to be shot again if:
    1. The shooter breaks the first bird and second bird is irregular.
    2. The shooter breaks the first bird and a malfunction of his gun or misfire prevents him shooting at his second bird.
    3. The shooter breaks the first bird but the second bird leaves late or not at all.
    4. The shooter breaks the first bird but the referee prevents the shooter from firing his second shot owing to the violation of *Article 3* providing the shooter has not already been warned for the same reason during the same round, otherwise the result of the first shot will be recorded and the second bird declared lost.
c) Zero and no bird, the double having, however, to be shot again if the shooter misses the first bird and the second bird is irregular for one of the reasons given under (b).

The regulations for *Articles 24* to *29, 33* and *34*, together with the regulations given under point (b) of *Article 32* are applicable to the shooting of doubles 'on the gun'. The last sentence does not apply to *Article 32*.

Ground Regulations

Article 36 All weapons, even unloaded, must be handled with the greatest care. The guns must be carried open; automatic guns must be carried with the breech open and the muzzle pointing upwards or downwards. Straps on guns are forbidden.

When the shooter is not using his gun it must be put vertically in a gun rack or in a similar place. It is forbidden to handle another shooter's gun without his permisison.

It is forbidden, during a competition or official championship, for two shooters to fire the same gun. In exceptional cases, owing to malfunctioning of his gun, it is permitted for the shooter to borrow, only during the round in which the incident occurs, the gun of another shooter.

Article 37 A shooter may only fire on his turn and only when a bird has been thrown. It is forbidden to aim or shoot at other shooters' targets. It is also forbidden to aim or shoot intentionally at living animals or birds.

No pretence of shooting is permitted on the shooting stand.

If a shooter, on the shooting stand before saying 'Ready', makes a pretence of shooting, a referee is obliged to issue a warning to the shooter. After this warning, any similar incident will lead to a zero score for the first target of the series which has been counted as successful.

Article 38 On roll call, the shooter must be ready to fire immediately and must take with him sufficient ammunition and equipment for the round.

Article 39 In no case must a shooter move to the stand before the preceding shooter has left it and it is his turn to shoot.

Article 40 The shooter is allowed to load his gun only when on the stand of the range when he has taken his place, his gun always pointing down the range and only when the referee has given the sign to start shooting.

Automatic guns must only be loaded with two cartridges.

Article 41 If the bird or birds of a double are not launched within the three seconds limit, the shooter has to signify that he does not want to shoot it or them by raising his gun in the air and not staying in the waiting position.

Article 42 The shooter must not turn around before he has broken his gun.

In the case of a no bird or if the shooting is interrupted, the gun must be opened. It can only be closed when firing resumes.

Article 43 In case of misfiring of malfunctioning of the gun or ammunition, the shooter has to remain where he is, the gun pointed down the range, not broken, and without touching the safety catch before the referee has examined the gun.

Article 44 The shooting must occur without interruption, the shooter being only allowed to pronounce the necessary words of command to announce 'Ready' or possibly to protest and to answer the referee's questions.

Article 45 The referee and his auxiliaries, under the control of the jury, see to the application of the rules, keep the onlookers out of the way and see that the shooters have a clear view from all the shooting stands.

Article 46 If the shooter or the team's captain does not agree with the referee about a shot, the complaint must be made immediately the incident occurs by raising the arm and saying 'protest' or 'appeal'.

The referee must then stop the shooting and after consulting his auxiliaries, give his decision. In no case will it be permissible to pick up a bird to see if it has been hit.

Article 47 The referee's decision may be brought up before the jury, either verbally or in writing.

If the jury finds the protest justified, they can give interaction to the referee for future judgements or elect a new referee or finally overrule the referee's decision. In no case must this decision concern knowing if a bird is killed or lost or knowing if the bird launched is defective, where no appeal can be made against the referee's decision.

Article 48 If a shooter or team's captain is of the opinion that the score announced at the end of the series is not correct, he must immediately make a complaint to the referee. The referee must then immediately and in the presence of the scorers check the result after which he makes his decision known. If the complainant does not agree with the decision, he has to present the jury with a short written protest.

Article 49 If a shooter or a team's captain or an official sees anything which is not according to the rules, he must advise the referee or a member of the jury.

If the referee cannot take immediate measures, he can refer the reporter to a member of the jury. Referee's decisions can be appealed against by means of a short written notice to a member of the jury.

Penalties, etc.

Article 50 All shooters are supposed to have acquainted themselves with the current regulations which apply to the shooting under Parcours de Chasse rules.

By taking part in the competition, they accept the penalties and other consequences resulting from violation of the rules and referee's orders.

Article 51 If the shooter uses jumps or ammunition not corresponding to the statements of *Articles 21* and *22* all shots fired with these weapons or ammunition are considered lost.

If the jury finds that the violation has been done intentionally, it can disqualify the shooter.

If however the jury finds the shooter could not be aware of the violation and has not gained a real advantage, it may decide to accept the result under condition that the fault is corrected and acknowledged.

Article 52 Violation of the rules first incurs a warning from the referee or a member of the jury.

In cases of further or more important offences the jury may fine the shooter with a lost bird or, in more serious cases, disqualify him from the round or even the competition.

Article 53 If a shooter does not present himself in his turn after being called three times, he will forfeit three birds taken from the first three killed birds of his following round. The jury may give him the opportunity to shoot his remaining birds later, at a time specified by the referee.

The shooter who refuses to act as auxiliary referee when this is required of him or obviously delays in taking up his position, will be penalised with the loss of a bird.

Article 54 If the jury notices a shooter deliberately delaying the competition or acting in a dishonest and dishonourable manner, it may give him a warning or fine him one bird or disqualify him from the competition.

Article 55 When the jury fines a shooter one bird and does not specify which one in particular, the first killed bird after the verdict must be considered as lost.

If the shooter has finished the day's shooting, the bird is deducted from the last round.

Tie Shooting

Article 56 If two or more shooters score the same results in a championship, the shoot off for the first three places will occur on new rounds of 25 birds until a difference shows up.

Shooting goes on according to the rules although squads need not consist of six shooters. If no time has been announced for the tie shoot those shooters concerned must remain in contact with the organisers in order to be able to start shooting not less than half an hour after the end of the ordinary competition.

Article 57 For the 4th and subsequent places precedence is decided by the scores in the last round.

Should this still result in a tie, the next to last round is considered, and so on. Finally, a decision may be reached by drawing lots.

Article 58 If two or more teams have the same score, and if no special rules have been put in the programme, the shooting will be held under the terms of *Article 56* between the teams to find the winners.

With regard to the other places, the shooting will be held in accordance with the terms of *Article 57*.

APPENDIX 1

The lists which follow give details of previous winners of the World and European FITASC championships.

They were provided by FITASC, Fédération Internationale de Tir aux Armes Sportives de Chasse, 10, Rue de Lisbonne, 75008 Paris, France.

World FITASC Champions

1979   Michel Riboulet (France)

1980   Michel Riboulet (France)

1981   Duncan Lawton (Great Britain)

1982   Marc Polet (Belgium)

1983   Michel Manjot (France)

1984   Gerry Cowler (Great Britain)

1985   Barry Simpson (Great Britain)

1986   Pascal Delaroche (France)

1987   A.J. Smith (Great Britain)

1988   John Bidwell (Great Britain)

1989   A.J. Smith (Great Britain)

1990   Mickey Rouse (Great Britain)

Women's World FITASC Champions

1979   Michele Roux (France)

1980   Anthea Hillyer (Great Britain)

1981   Claude Meng (France)

1982   Anthea Hillyer (Great Britain)

1983   Anthea Hillyer (Great Britain)

1984   Denise Eyre (Great Britain)

1985   Ghislaine Batut (France)

1986   Anthea Hillyer (Great Britain)

1987   Denise Eyre (Great Britain)

1988   Anthea Hillyer (Great Britain)

1989   Denise Eyre (Great Britain)

1990   Anthea Hillyer (Great Britain)

European FITASC Champions

1968   Henri Boucher (France)

1969   Francis Leurkin (Belgium)

1970   W.J. Skyes (Great Britain)

1971   W.J. Skyes (Great Britain)

1972   Michel Riboulet (France)

1973   Luciano Brunetti (Italy)

1974   Michel Jousse (France)

1975   Brian Hebditch (Great Britain)

1976   Marc Polet (Belgium)

1977   Brian Wells (Great Britain)

1978   Brian Wells (Great Britain)

1979   Paddy Howe (Great Britain)

1980   Paddy Howe (Great Britain)

1981   Michel Riboulet (France)

1982   Duncan Lawton (Great Britain)

1983   Michel Come (France)

1984   A.J. Smith (Great Britain)

1985   J. Marie Cloquemin (France)

1986   Barry Simpson (Great Britain)

1987   A.J. Smith (Great Britain)

1988   Duane Morley (Great Britain)

1989   A.J. Smith (Great Britain)

1990   Mickey Rouse (Great Britain)

Women's European FITASC Champions

1968   J. Harang (France)

1969   J. Harang (France)

1970   Marguerite Delbats (France)

1971   Marguerite Delbats (France)

1972   Jocelyne Pizani (France)

1973   Mme De Meester (France)

1974   Mme De Meester (France)

1975   Mme Legrelle (Belgium)

1976   Mme Legrelle (Belgium)

1977   Michele Roux (France)

1978   Michele Roux (France)

1979   Michele Roux (France)

1980   Anthea Hillyer (Great Britain)

1981   Claude Meng (France)

1982   Michele Roux (France)

1983   Anthea Hillyer (Great Britain)

1984   Gudrun Pfitzer (Germany)

1985   Gudrun Pfitzer (Germany)

1986   Denise Eyre (Great Britain)

1987   Jane Blot (France)

1988   Ruth Leah (Great Britain)

1989   Denise Eyre (Great Britain)

1990   Ruth Leah (Great Britain)

APPENDIX 2

GLOSSARY

ABT Automatic ball trap, an international trap discipline which is especially popular in France.

Averages Published annually by the Clay Pigeon Shooting Association, they record members' scores in the eight main disciplines and classify them according to their ability.

Battue Usually a testing clay target which travels very fast and drops just as quickly. It often flies edge-on to the shooter.

Choke A constriction at the muzzle end of a barrel designed to vary the size and density of the shot pattern.

CPSA The Clay Pigeon Shooting Association, the governing body of clay shooting in the United Kingdom.

Crossers Very common target from the right or left in English and FITASC Sporting.

Doubles Targets thrown in pairs, either on report, following or simultaneously.

Double Rise Trap shooting derived from DTL in which two targets are thrown simultaneously.

Double Trap Newest of the trap disciplines and originally designed specifically for the Olympic Games.

Driven A target thrown towards the shooter to simulate the flight of a 'driven' bird, such as grouse or pheasant in the field.

DTL Down the Line, the simplest and most straightforward of the trap disciplines. It requires great concentration to shoot successfully at the top level.

FITASC	Fédération International de Tir aux Armes Sportives de Chasse, the ruling body of International Sporting.
Gun Position	Whether the gun is in or out of the shoulder when the target is called for. In FITASC, the gun must be down until the target is visible.
ISU	International Shooting Union, the governing body of the Olympic shooting disciplines for shotgun, rifle and pistol.
Incomer	A target that is released towards the shooter.
Lead	The distance the moving gun barrels must be in front of a target in order to compensate for its speed and kill it.
Midi	A 90mm clay target which flies fast and straight. Regarded by many shooters as the most consistent of all the clay targets.
Mini	A 60mm clay target which initially travels much faster than a standard clay but slows down very quickly.
Mounting	The act of bringing the gun into your shoulder before firing.
No Bird	An irregular target.
NSCA	National Sporting Clays Association of America.
OT	Olympic Trap, also known as Fifteen Trap. One of the most demanding of the clay shooting disciplines with fast, angled targets.
Rabbit	A target designed for rolling along the ground from a special trap.
Report	An 'on report' target is the second one of a pair and is only released after the gun is fired at the first target.
Rocket	Widely used in FITASC Sporting, the rocket flies deceptively slowly and is hard to break because of its thickness.
Skeet	A discipline in which targets are shot in a set sequence of singles and doubles from high and low trap houses. There are two versions of skeet and the international one is an Olympic discipline.
Skeet Vest	A sleeveless jacket with large pockets specially designed for all forms of clay shooting.
Squad	A pre-selected number of shooters grouped either by draw or computer to compete together in a competition.

Teal   Usually known as springing teal, this is a fast rising target found on most Sporting layouts.

Traps   The mechanical devices used to throw the various targets.

UT   Universal Trench, also known as Five Trap. Another exacting trap disicipline.

USSCA   United States Sporting Clays Association.

INDEX